Discover the world's best destinations with the Insight Guides Walking Eye app, available to download for free in the App Store and Google Play.

The container app provides easy access to fantastic free content on events and activities taking place in your current location or chosen destination, with the possibility of booking, as well as the regularly-updated Insight Guides travel blog: Inspire Me. In addition, you can purchase curated, premium destination guides through the app, which feature local highlights, hotel, bar, restaurant and shopping listings, an A to Z of practical information and more. Or purchase and download Insight Guides eBooks straight to your device.

INSIGHT ⊙ GUIDES

Walking Eye

⊙ **DESTINATIONS**

⊘ **INSPIRE ME**

▥ **EBOOKS**

▦ **EVENTS**

TOP 10 ATTRACTIONS

BINIBECA VELL
A 'fishermen's village' designed for tourists. See page 80.

ESGLÉSIA DE SANTA MARIA
Famed for its grand organ and one of the sights in the capital, Maó. See page 30.

PLAÇA D'ES BORN
This square in Ciutadella is surrounded by some splendid mansions. See page 59.

CALA SANTA GALDANA
A lovely cove, popular with families and watersports enthusiasts. See page 72.

CIUTADELLA
The golden walls of the town rise above the harbour. See page 57.

PARC NATURAL DE S'ALBUFERA
A haven for birdwatching and exploring the coastal environment. See page 40.

FORNELLS
A pretty harbour and some tempting fish restaurants. See page 45.

NAVETA D'ES TUDONS
Believed to be the oldest roofed building in Europe. See page 56.

ES MERCADAL
A delightful inland town that specialises in island food – *cuina menorquina*. See page 51.

CALA EN TURQUETA
One of the many lovely little coves in the south of the island. See page 71.

A PERFECT DAY

9.00am

Breakfast

Enjoy a typically Menorcan breakfast of fresh orange juice, good coffee and sugar-dusted *ensaimadas* in Es Llonguet (Carrer del Rosari 12), near the harbour.

11.30am

Exploring the harbour

You may want to buy some Menorcan sandals *(abarcas)* in one of the shops on Carrer Ses Moreres before making your way down the broad steps of the Costa de Ses Voltes, stopping to admire the view of the harbour as you go.

10.00am

Market in the Claustre del Carme

Visit the morning market in the Claustre del Carme, where glistening fresh fruit and vegetables are piled up beside stalls selling jewellery, household items and some delicious speciality foods.

1pm

Concert

Go to the Església de Santa Maria in the Plaça de Sa Constitució for the organ concert that takes place daily except Sunday (June–Oct).

3.30pm

A boat trip

Take a trip around the harbour in a glass-bottomed boat. A recorded commentary will point out the Illa del Lazaret, which used to be a quarantine centre, the dramatic bulk of the Fortaleza de la Mola and Golden Farm, wrongly but romantically associated with Lord Nelson and Lady Emma Hamilton.

2.30pm

Lunch

You will be spoiled for choice when choosing where to go for lunch, but elegant La Minerva (Moll de Levant 87, tel: 971 351 995), although expensive, offers an excellent-value tasting menu, and the opportunity to eat outside on a floating jetty – bliss.

10.30pm

Dinner

Head to the friendly Nou Siroco restaurant (it's best to book, tel: 971 367 965) back at the harbour for a late dinner – the paella is good – or to sample a wide selection of tapas for which the restaurant is well known.

5.00pm

Es Castell and Cales Fonts

Once back on dry land, walk to the far end of the harbour and up a small hill, where you can catch a bus to nearby Es Castell. You can explore this pleasant and still very British-influenced little town and then, as the sun goes down, have an evening drink or two by the waterside in pretty little Cales Fonts.

CONTENTS

INTRODUCTION

Menorca is an appealing little island. It has neither the dramatic visual appeal of Mallorca's vertiginous coastline nor the brashness of Ibiza's nightlife, but it offers considerable diversity in a very small area – from the rugged, wind-swept stretches of the undeveloped north coast, to the stunningly beautiful bays in the south; plus the pleasures of two handsome, historic cities. All this is what keeps visitors coming back year after year, and the reason that estate agents are flourishing, selling second-home properties to English enthusiasts. In 1993, the island was declared a Unesco Biosphere Reserve – a distinction of which Menorcans are extremely proud. It means that the whole island is under some form of protection, although only S'Albufera d'es Grau is a designated Parc Natural.

Unesco reserve

A Biosphere Reserve is defined by Unesco as 'a place of important natural and cultural heritage where economic development is compatible with nature conservation'. One of the objectives of the reserve is to control the negative impacts of tourism, which means that no uncontrolled development can take place, although responsible tourism is welcomed.

GEOGRAPHY

Menorca lies just 225km (140 miles) southeast of Barcelona – from where there are regular ferry and air services. It is the second largest of the Balearic group – after Mallorca – but it is still tiny, only 47km (30 miles) from east to west, and some 20km (12 miles) from north to south at its widest point. Roughly 215km (135 miles) of coastline encircle the island, but there is no road to take you all the way around it – you often have to return to the central axis. The island is fairly flat, and the highest point, Monte Toro, crowned by a sanctuary, reaches only 358m (1,170ft).

Macarella beach and cove on the island's south coast

LANDSCAPE AND VEGETATION

The main road that spans the island, linking the two cities, also roughly divides two distinct geological zones. The northern section is sandstone, with bare rocks and reddish earth; small fields are enclosed by dry-stone walls *(parets seques)*, among which ancient olive trees, myrtle and juniper bushes are rooted, but there is little sign of cultivation. Farming here has always been arduous, and many people abandoned it when tourism offered an alternative. Much of the land in the north of the island is covered by dense scrub known as *maquis*, with heather and rosemary present as well.

The southern part of the island is characterised by limestone karst, cut through by lush ravines running down to the sea. The centre is a fertile region of low, gently undulating hills, dotted with neat farmsteads, surrounded by meadows, groves of Aleppo pine, carob trees and stands of holm oak. Few crops, except olives, are produced in any viable quantity, but the dairy industry, introduced by the British, still flourishes, and herds of black-and-white cows, which can be seen grazing the fields, provide milk from which to make the local cheese, Queso de Mahón, still made in the traditional way (see page 103).

If you visit Menorca in late summer or autumn, you may be struck by the lack of vegetation. But come in spring and you will find large parts of the island covered in wild flowers, including foxgloves, violets and daisies, the spiky-bloomed asphodel and several varieties of wild orchids. Apparently inhospitable areas turn bright yellow with broom, and pink-and-white rock roses bloom well into summer. The evergreen mastic tree, from which a rubbery resin, used in making varnish, is extracted, has a reddish bloom.

BIRDLIFE

Menorca is a convenient stopping off point for thousands of migrant birds in spring and autumn, and it also has a diverse resident population. In the marshland areas of the Parc Natural S'Albufera d'es Grau herons and cattle egrets are commonly seen, along with other waders, while booted eagles wheel overhead, and kites and buzzards have their nests along the rocky coast nearby. The Barranc d'Algendar is the place to hear nightingales and see skies filled with alpine swifts; colourful bee-eaters can often be spotted around the coastal dunes.

CLIMATE

Summer temperatures in Menorca average 24ºC (76ºF) but highs of over 30ºC (86ºF) are not unusual. Water temperature in mid-summer never drops below 20ºC (68ºF). Winter months of November to February are the wettest, and the time when the Tramuntana wind blows most fiercely, especially on the north coast. May and September/October are months of pleasantly warm temperatures and fewer visitors.

POPULATION AND LANGUAGE

The population numbers around 91,000 – about a tenth of Mallorca's total – of which some 29,000 live in the capital, Maó, and a similar number in Ciutadella. These two cities are distinct in character, moulded over the centuries by the different occupying forces: the British in Maó; the Spanish in Ciutadella. Both now make their living chiefly from tourism, as does some 56 percent of the island's population. Strung out between the two cities, a few small, pretty towns retain traditional industries, chiefly the production of leather goods and cheese.

Menorcans are bilingual in Spanish and Menorquí, a variant of Catalan, which is now the official language. Most people speak Menorquí among themselves, but they all speak Castilian (Spanish), too, and, while they are delighted if foreign visitors know a few words of Menorquí, they don't expect it. Signs and street names are mostly written in Menorquí, although some seem to swerve between the two languages. Some towns have been renamed, and older maps may still give the original, Spanish name.

GETTING AROUND THE ISLAND

Most of Menorca's beaches are in the south. Some are tiny, idyllic coves, accessible only on foot through pine woods or by a bumpy

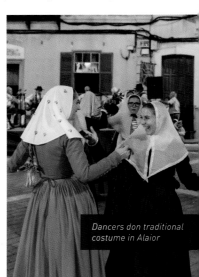

Dancers don traditional costume in Alaior

car journey over unmade roads. Others are long, broad sweeps of white sand, around which hotels and villa complexes have mushroomed, offering everything visitors need or desire – sometimes at the expense of the area's natural beauty.

As there is no coastal road, drivers have to keep returning to the main central highway (Me-1), on the series of roads that radiate out from it. There is a coastal path, called the Camí de Cavalls (Horses' Way), which was constructed for military patrols in the Middle Ages and which has now been fully renovated and reopened for walkers – with parts of it open to horse riders and mountain bikers, too.

REASONS TO VISIT

Visitors to Menorca – of whom some 30 percent are from the UK, with Germans forming the largest group – come for a wide variety of reasons. Families with young children appreciate the safe beaches and warm Mediterranean waters and the facilities that have grown up around them but which have not attracted the 'lager lout' tourists that have given Menorca's sister islands a bad name.

Water sports enthusiasts are attracted by the ideal windsurfing conditions, especially on the north coast around Fornells, and by opportunities for scuba diving in the clear coastal waters.

Walkers love the peaceful paths around the island's coasts and the slightly more challenging ones through the lush central gorges – the *barrancos*, while birdwatchers form flocks of their own during the spring and autumn migratory seasons, especially in S'Albufera des Grau.

Visitors interested in the ancient past delight in the wealth of prehistoric sites – about 1,000 of them – which comprise *talyots* (cylindrical stone watchtowers), *taules* (T-shaped structures probably used for sacrifice and other ritual purposes) and *navetas* (huge, stone-built communal tombs).

Other people come here to explore the historic cities of Maó and Ciutadella, which both have splendid harbours, elegant architecture, atmospheric cobbled streets, some smart shops, a smattering of museums and a plethora of good restaurants. Despite their popularity, these cities have maintained the atmosphere of small friendly towns.

Those who enjoy traditional *fiestas* try to time their visits to coincide with the wild celebrations of the Festes de Gràcia in Maó in early September, or the Festa de Sant Joan in mid-June in Ciutadella (see pages 96 and 97). Come to Menorca and discover which of these varied aspects appeals most to you.

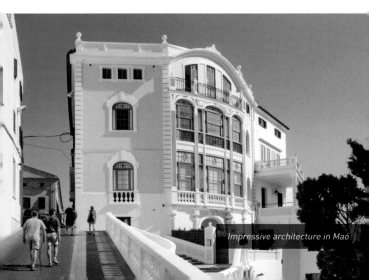

Impressive architecture in Maó

A BRIEF HISTORY

Menorca is an island with a long history. A number of settlers and invaders have taken control and made their mark before being usurped by a more forceful power, and their diverse influences have shaped this small island, leaving lasting monuments and intriguing idiosyncrasies.

PREHISTORIC PEOPLE

During the Bronze Age, between 3000 and 1300BC, the island was inhabited by people who probably came from the Iberian peninsula. Cave dwellings can be seen in the south – Cales Coves and Cova d'es Colom – and in the north at Cala Morell.

Taula at Torralba d'en Salort

Towards the end of this period these early people built *navetes*, so-called because they were shaped like inverted ships (*navis* is Latin for ship). They were communal ossuaries, used to bury bones once the flesh had decomposed in some other (unknown) site. The best known of these is the Naveta d'es Tudons, near Ciutadella.

The first settlers were superseded by people of the *Talayotic* culture, named after the stone towers called *talayots* built as part of their settlements. Around 200 have survived; among the most spectacular are those at Talati de Dalt, Torre d'en Galmes and Trepucó while the best-preserved settlements are Son Catlar, in the southwest, and Sant Agustí Vell, near Sant Tomás. The other remarkable legacy

> **Roman remains**
>
> Archaeologists are currently excavating the ruins of the Roman settlement of Sanisera (Sanitja), at Cap de Cavalleria, which has only recently been discovered (see page 47).

of the period are the *taules* – T-shaped stone structures composed of two massive stone slabs that are believed to be sites of ritual sacrifice. The most impressive can be seen at the sites mentioned above, and at Torralba d'en Salort and Torre Trencada.

CARTHAGINIANS AND ROMANS

Over the centuries, Phoenicians, Carthaginians and Greeks traded with the Balearic Islands and (around 400BC) the Carthaginians gradually colonised them, absorbed them into their trading empire and founded the main ports. The colonisers found that the islanders' skill with stones was not confined to construction work but was also evident in their deadly use of the slingshot. The 'Balearic slingers' were recruited by Hannibal to fight for the Carthaginians in the Punic Wars. The name Balearic probably comes from the Greek word, ballein, meaning 'to throw'.

The Carthaginians were soon superseded as the ruling force: by 123BC the Romans had pacified most of Spain and sent out a force to conquer the islands, which they named Balearis Major (Mallorca) and Balearis Minor (Menorca). They built roads, such as the one that can still be seen at Puig de Santa Agueda, and established ports: Port Magonum (Maó), Jammo (Ciutadella) and Sanisera (Sanitja). Some early Christian basilicas survive from the end of the era, most notably Son Bou and Fornás de Torelló, which has a magnificent paved mosaic.

After the collapse of the Roman Empire, the Balearics were subjected to continuous plundering, chiefly by the Vandals (c.AD425) who destroyed most traces of Roman civilisation. The next rulers to give any sense of continuity were the Moors; a Moorish army had landed on the Iberian peninsula in 711 and in just seven years, most of Spain was under Moorish rule. At first the caliphs (rulers) were content simply to accept tribute from Mallorca and Menorca, but local disturbances prompted them to invade and, despite strong resistance, both islands were conquered at the beginning of the 10th century, when they became part of the Caliphate of Córdoba. In c.1080 the islands became a separate emirate, under more aggressive rulers. Very little Moorish architecture survived the early 13th-century Christian conquest, but the legacy can be seen and heard in many place names – those with the prefix Al-, such as Alaior, or Bin-, such as Binibecca and Binmel-là.

THE RECONQUEST

Following the recovery of Jerusalem in 1099 it took 400 years of sieges and battles before Christian rulers succeeded in subduing the Moors. The crusades in Spain were aimed at the eviction of the ruling Muslims and the recapture of all Spanish lands. In 1229, a Catalan army led by King Jaume I of Aragón and Catalunya took Mallorca. The Moors who remained were forcibly converted to Christianity, but Jaume proved to be an enlightened ruler. The Moors on Menorca agreed to pay an annual tribute and were left in peace until 1287, when the long and largely beneficial reign of Jaume I was followed by dynastic rivalry, and the brutal Alfonso III of Aragón found a pretext for invasion. The Moors were defeated and expelled or killed. After

Alfonso's death, Jaume II, a wiser ruler, stimulated trade in the Balearics. In the 14th century, Menorca's economy prospered, but when trade routes to the East were cut by the Turks in the mid-15th century, things went seriously downhill.

THE GOLDEN AGE

In 1492, the newly unified Spain under the Catholic Monarchs, Ferdinand and Isabella, completed the reconquest, taking Granada, the only Moorish enclave left on the Iberian peninsula. In the same year, Christopher Columbus, funded by the Spanish Crown, sailed across the Atlantic. Over the subsequent century and a half, known as the Golden Age, Spain imposed its language, culture and religion on the Americas, creating a vast empire. Conquistadors extracted vast riches in silver and gold, but, plagued by corruption and incompetence and drained of manpower and ships by such adventurism as the dispatch of the Armada against England in 1588, Spain was unable to defend her interests.

The Balearic Islands did not share in the riches of these years. For them, this was a period of great instability. Along with Catalunya, they were forbidden to trade with the New World, and their existing trade eastwards was interrupted by pirate raids

A monument to Alfonso III stands in Maó

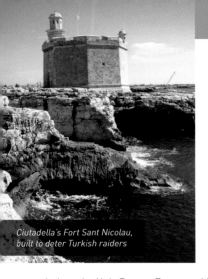

Ciutadella's Fort Sant Nicolau, built to deter Turkish raiders

and attacks by the powerful Turkish fleet. These incursions culminated in the devastation of Maó in 1535 and, after a bitter 10-day siege, of Ciutadella, in 1558. The fortress of Sant Felip at the entrance to the port of Maó and the imposing Fort Sant Nicolau in Ciutadella were built in response to these attacks.

CHANGING FORTUNES

The daughter of Ferdinand and Isabella married the heir to the Holy Roman Emperor, Maximilian of Habsburg. The Spanish crown duly passed to the Habsburgs and remained in their hands until the feeble-minded Carlos II died childless in 1700. France seized the chance to install the grandson of Louis XIV on the Spanish throne. A rival Habsburg claimant was supported by Austria and Britain, who feared a powerful Spanish-French alliance. In the subsequent War of the Spanish Succession (1702–13) most of the kingdom of Aragón, including the Balearics, backed the Habsburgs.

Aware of the importance of Maó's harbour, Britain seized Menorca in 1708 and retained it, under the Treaty of Utrecht, once the war was over. One of the most lasting British acts was to make Maó the capital, instead of Ciutadella. Relations with the occupiers were fairly harmonious; under the first British governor, Sir Richard Kane a road was built to link the two cities, and the economy was improved and strengthened. In 1756, at the beginning of the Seven Years' War, French troops captured the island. They founded the town of Sant Lluís (near Maó), but their occupation was short-lived: under the Treaty of Paris in 1763, Menorca was returned to the British.

In order to repel a further attack, numerous fortifications were built, including the Georgetown garrison, later to become Villa Carlos, now Es Castell. Despite this, in 1781, when Spain was aligned with France, Franco-Spanish troops landed on Menorca, and the island fell to Spain. During the next few years the Spaniards destroyed the fort of Sant Felip and (in 1795) established the diocese of Menorca, with Ciutadella as its bishopric. The British briefly regained the island in 1798 but, under the Treaty of Amiens in 1802, relinquished it to Spain once and for all.

The economy fell into a poor state during the 19th century, and numerous Menorcans emigrated to Algeria, South

◎ SIR RICHARD KANE

The first British governor of Menorca, Sir Richard Kane (1660–1736), was a resourceful and capable man. He drained marshes, introduced Friesian cattle and new varieties of fruit, stimulated the wine industry and financed the water cistern at Es Mercadel. Most importantly, he commissioned the construction of the first connecting road between Maó and Ciutadella, the Camí d'en Kane, some 16km (10 miles) of which still survive (see page 51). It was largely due to his leadership that relations between the islanders and colonisers were so good during the first period of British rule, and he is still remembered with affection.

America and the US. What commercial success was engendered through the wine industry ended when the phylloxera louse destroyed the island's vines at the end of the century.

REPUBLIC AND CIVIL WAR

The early 20th century in Spain was marked by social and political crises, assassinations and near anarchy, culminating, in 1921, in a coup and the dictatorship of General Primo de Rivera. He fell in 1929, and when elections of 1931 revealed massive anti-royalist feeling, the king followed him into exile. The new Republic was conceived amid an outbreak of strikes and uprisings. In February 1936 the left-wing Popular Front won a majority of seats in the Cortes (parliament), but across Spain localised violence displaced debate.

In July 1936, General Francisco Franco staged a coup, which was supported by the military, monarchists, conservatives, the clergy and the right-wing Falangist Movement. Aligned on the Republican government's side were liberals, socialists, communists and anarchists. The ensuing Civil War (1936–9) was brutal and bitter, and during the three years it lasted, around one million Spaniards lost their lives.

Sadly, Mallorca and Menorca found themselves on opposite sides. While Mallorca's garrison seized the island for the Nationalists, Menorca declared for the Republic, and stayed with it to the bitter end – it proved to be the last Republican stronghold in Spain.

TRANSFORMATION AND DEMOCRACY

Spain remained on the sidelines during World War II, and, after the dark years of isolation known as the *Noche Negra* (Black Night), began a slow economic recovery, boosted by the growth of the tourism industry.

In the late 1950s and early 1960s northern Europeans began visiting Spain and the Balearic Islands in significant numbers. The first charter plane landed in Menorca in 1953, and within two decades a trickle of visitors had grown to half a million. Throughout Spain, tourism helped transform the impoverished country's economy and landscape, as well as influencing society by introducing liberal ideas. Eager to capitalise, both the government and private interests poured everything into mass tourism, triggering a rash of uncontrolled, indiscriminate building. Mallorca and Ibiza experienced an explosive growth in tourism, but Menorca came more slowly to the industry and remained more low key.

When Franco died in 1975, his chosen successor, enthroned as Juan Carlos I, managed a smooth transition to democracy: new

Tourists on the beach in 1966

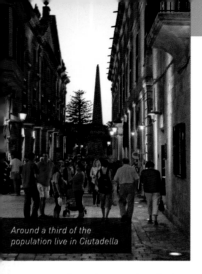
Around a third of the population live in Ciutadella

freedoms were granted to Spanish regions, whose languages and cultures enjoyed a renaissance. The Balearics obtained a degree of autonomy in 1978 and five years later became an autonomous community.

MENORCA TODAY

In 1986 Spain joined the EEC (now the European Union, or EU), which further boosted the economy. In 1993, Unesco declared Menorca a Biosphere Reserve. Over the next decade the economy prospered, but there was increasing concern about accelerating tourist resort development, as well as the high price of land, pushed up by foreign ownership. The island government has taken steps to limit the damage inflicted by mass tourism. Strict building regulations have been imposed and a natural park created to protect the land around S'Albufera d'es Grau. Menorca has learned much from the mistakes made by its neighbours, and most visitors to this lovely island will be pleasantly surprised at how little despoliation there is, and how much of its traditions, culture and natural beauty have been preserved.

The recession that affected most of Europe (and the US) in the first decade of the 21st century meant that tourist numbers dropped and businesses suffered. However, the islands' economies have rebounded in recent years, with a record number – over 15 million – visiting the Balearic Islands in 2016.

HISTORICAL LANDMARKS

3000–1300BC Menorca populated by cave dwellers who build *navetes*.

1300–123BC *Talayotic* culture, named after the towers called *talayots*.

400BC Carthaginians conquer and colonise the Balearics.

123BC Romans defeat Carthaginians and name the island Balearis Minor; under Roman rule Christianity is established and towns founded.

848 Moorish Caliphs of Spain quell disturbances in the Balearics and impose Islam; Moorish rule in the Balearics lasts for 300 years.

1229 After Palma de Mallorca falls to the Christian army, Menorca agrees to pay tribute to Aragón.

1285–7 Alfonso III invades Menorca.

1492 Spain united under Ferdinand and Isabella.

1708 Menorca is taken by the British in the War of the Spanish Succession.

1722 British shift the capital from Ciutadella to Maó.

1756–63 French occupy Menorca until it is handed back to the British under Treaty of Paris.

1781 Franco-Spanish troops take Menorca.

1802 The Treaty of Amiens gives the island to Spain

1936–9 Civil War. Menorca declares for the Republic.

1936–75 Franco's dictatorship, with the early years typified by economic hardship; in the 1960s, tourism starts to bring prosperity.

1975 King Juan Carlos I enthroned after the death of Franco.

1978 Statute of Autonomy. In 1983, Balearic Islands become an autonomous province and Menorquí is restored as official language.

1986 Spain joins European Economic Community (now European Union).

2002 The euro becomes the currency of Spain.

2011 The right-of-centre Partido Popular (PP) takes power.

2014 King Juan Carlos I abdicates in favour of Felipe VI.

2016 Balearic government introduces a tourist tax (up to €2 per day) to finance sustainable tourism projects across the islands.

2017 The left-wing coalition government introduces compulsory licenses to rent apartments to tourists and announces plans to double the tourism tax as of 2018.

Gleaming white Binibeca Vell

WHERE TO GO

Most visitors to Menorca arrive at the neat Sant Climent airport, approximately 5km (3 miles) south of the capital, Maó. Others come by sea from Barcelona to the terminals in Maó or Ciutadella, or hop over from Mallorca on a short ferry trip. Once here, getting round the island is not a problem; hiring a car obviously gives you a greater degree of freedom, but if you are based in either of the two cities, you will be able to use the regular and reliable bus service to reach most points of interest. What is more difficult is travelling between resorts by public transport.

A single busy main road, the Me-1, punctuated by a handful of small towns, runs through the gently undulating landscape, linking Maó in the east and Ciutadella in the west – a distance of 47km (30 miles). A network of minor roads leads to the wetlands of S'Albufera d'es Grau and the port of Fornells in the craggy northeast, and to the idyllic coves and long sandy beaches in the south. At present there is no road running all the way round the coast: you must return to the central axis between destinations. Some minor roads are poor but have been improved enormously in recent years.

MAÓ

Maó ❶, the largest town, with a population of around 29,000, is the business and administrative capital of Menorca but above all, it is a port. The 5km (3-mile) long, deep-water natural harbour, guarded by forts and shielded by surrounding hills, caught the eye of the British Navy early in the 18th century. In 1708, during the War of the Spanish Succession, the British seized the island and kept it until 1802, excepting two periods:

Maó's picturesque harbour

they relinquished it to the French between 1756 and 1763, and the Spanish held it for 16 years from 1782. The British shifted the capital from Ciutadella to Maó, and built a road between the two. Their occupation left its mark in a number of ways: they introduced gin and the dairy industry to the island, and both have flourished ever since. They also introduced sash windows to Maó – a rare thing in the Mediterranean.

AROUND THE PLAÇA DE S'ESPLANADA

The streets of the old city are narrow, and many are pedestrianised, so the only way to explore it is on foot. If you drive into town, park in the underground car park (Mon–Sat 8.30am–10pm) in the large, palm-lined **Plaça de s'Esplanada Ⓐ**, which was formerly used by the British as a parade ground. If you come by bus, you'll be dropped off at the terminus to the west of the square. Old people sit chatting on stone benches, and children clamber and swing in a little playground, but despite some elegant buildings (among which stands a Burger King), it is not a particularly remarkable square. An obelisk commemorates those who fell in the Spanish Civil War (1936–39), and soldiers guard the still-operational barracks behind it. As the monument refers only to those who died on the Nationalist side, it is not uncommon to see it embellished with graffiti. On Tuesdays and Saturdays a huge market occupies the centre of the square.

Just off the eastern side of the square, in Carrer Sa Rovellada de Dalt, is the **Ateneu Cientific, Leterari i Artístic** (www.ateneu mao.org; Mon–Fri 10am–2pm and 4–10pm, Sat 10am–2pm; free), an old-fashioned place that is home to Menorca's most important cultural association. It contains a library, and a collection of landscapes, still lifes, ceramic plates and wall tiles. You will have to ask if you want to see the ante-chamber, which is full of stuffed native birds, fish in formalin, seashells and minerals that are kept under lock and key.

The Carrer de Ses Morreres, a busy shopping street with some smart boutiques, runs from the **plaça** towards the old town and the port. A bust commemorates Dr Mateo José Orfila (1787–1853), who was born at No. 13 and went on to found modern toxicology and pathology in the Institut Pasteur in Paris. At the intersection with Carrer de Bastió, where a sinuously curved first-floor window grabs the attention, the street becomes

House of Hanover

Carrer Hannover (the spelling is intentional) was named in honour of the Hanoverian regiment garrisoned in the Plaça de s'Esplanada during the first period of British occupation (1708–56). It is a reminder that during these years the British throne was occupied by members of the House of Hanover.

The Ajuntament (Town Hall) in Maó

the pedestrianised Carrer Hannover (also called Costa de Sa Plaça).

THE CENTRAL PLAÇA

There are more shopping opportunities here, before the road passes through little Plaça de Colón, with a statue of a young girl adorning a fountain, and an excellent bookshop, and you reach the **Plaça de Sa Constitució**, which is dominated by the great **Església de Santa Maria B** (Mon–Fri 7.45am–1pm and 4–8.30pm, Sat 7.45am–1pm, Sun 8.30am–12.30pm; free). Founded by Alfonso III shortly after his victory over the Moors in 1287, it was rebuilt in the mid-18th century, when the British controlled the island. It is an eclectic mixture of architectural styles. The facade is neoclassical, the single-aisled nave is pure Catalan Gothic and the great altar is embellished with Baroque and rococo flourishes. The most renowned object in the church is the mighty organ, with 3,210 pipes; a masterpiece of its kind, it was commissioned from a renowned Swiss organ-maker in 1809. Between June and October, half-hour concerts are held from Monday to Saturday at 1pm (small entrance fee), and it is lovely to sit and listen to the music swelling around you, while you take time to examine some of the details of the church.

Another imposing building in the square, the **Ajuntament** (Town Hall), was built on the site of a medieval fortress, but very little survives from the earlier structure. The facade is crowned by a bell wall and clock tower, which was donated to the city by the first British governor, Sir Richard Kane (see page 21). The huge male and female figures outside the main council chamber wearing Menorcan folk dress are carried through the streets of Maó during festivals.

SANT ROC AND SANT FRANCESC

Opposite the Town Hall, Carrer de Sant Roc leads to the late 15th-century **Port de Sant Roc**, the only one of Maó's mighty medieval town gates surviving from the original fortifications. In a niche above it is a sculpture of Sant Roc, who is believed to have saved Maó from a plague outbreak. A few yards to the left is the Plaça del Bastió, with restaurants and cafés surrounding a children's play area in the centre.

Turning right from the gate, along Carrer des Rector Mort, through what used to be the smartest suburb of Maó, you reach Carrer d'Isabel II (which you could also have followed from the Town Hall). At the far end of this street you'll come to the Plaça d'es Monestir and the **Parròquia de Sant Francesc d'Assís** 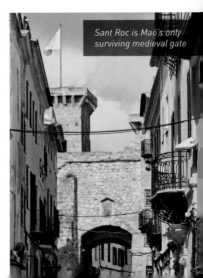 (guided tour in English: June–Sept, Tue 7.30pm). Completed in 1792, after many years' work, this was the church of a Franciscan monastery, founded in the mid-15th

Sant Roc is Maó's only surviving medieval gate

century. Although the entrance doorway looks Romanesque, it is in fact Renaissance. Inside, a 19th-century *grisaille* wall painting illustrates scenes from the life of St Francis; the Chapel of the Immaculate Conception is decorated in highly ornamental Churrigueresque style.

All that remains of the former monastery is the elegant cloister, which houses the extensive historical and archaeological collections of the **Museu de Menorca** (June–Sept Tue–Sat 10am–2pm, 6–8pm, Sun 10am–2pm, Oct–May Tue and Thu 10am–6pm, Wed, Fri and Sat–Sun 10am–2pm). Exhibits range from *talayotic* finds to Greek and Roman amphorae, Islamic tiles, Spanish and British ceramics – the Spanish ones are most attractive – and 20th-century paintings, while modern sculpture is displayed in the courtyard.

The striking Sant Francesc now houses the Museu de Menorca

CARRER D'ISABEL II AND PLAÇA DE LA CONQUISTA

Retracing your steps along Carrer d'Isabel II you will pass a number of places of interest, including a narrow alley leading through whitewashed arches down to the port and the colonial-style palace of the former British governor, today the seat of the Gobierno Militar. You will also pass several smart mansions with Georgian doorways and sash windows, as well as a wonderful candle shop, the Cereria Abella, before arriving back at the Town Hall.

Turn left down the narrow Carrer Alfons II and you will find yourself on the other side of the huge church of Santa Maria, in Plaça de la Conquista. Here, the patrician house called Ca'n Mercadal contains the main Menorcan library, a monument to Alfonso III stands outside the rear entrance to the church and just round the corner an interesting shop, at No. 9, Portal de Mar sells antiques and gifts. From the end of a cul-de-sac called Carrer d'Alfons III there is a fabulous view across the harbour.

CARRER NOU TO CLAUSTRE DEL CARME

From Plaça de Sa Constitució, follow Carrer Nou, a bustling, pedestrianised shopping street, to Plaça Reial, a little square packed with café tables. Going west, up Costa d'en Deià, you come to the arched entrance to the **Parc d'es Freginal** (daily 8am–8pm; free), a city park that offers a shady green refuge from the summer heat, and has a children's play area. It really comes into its own in the days before the Festa de la Vierge de Gràcia (7–9 Sept; see page 96), when jazz concerts are held here.

Just around the corner is the well-renovated **Teatre Principal**, in front of which is a large bronze statue of muse Talia, holding the comedy and tragedy masks. Italian architect and operatic tenor Giovanni Pelaggi designed the original building, and the curtain first rose here in 1829. Apart from Opera Week (during Semana Santa, the week preceding Easter), little remains of the glorious days of opera, when Italian ensembles began their tours of Spain in Maó, but there is a full programme of performances, including classical concerts, and Latin American music (see page 95).

Going east, from the Plaça Reial, along Carrer Sa Ravaleta, another good shopping street, you will soon come to the huge 18th-century Església del Carme and its adjoining cloister, the **Claustre del Carme D**. The cloister was confiscated and deconsecrated in 1835, like most monastic property in Spain, and after serving a number of secular purposes it was transformed into the city market in the 1980s. Alongside fresh produce stalls are others selling speciality foods, jewellery, shoes and gifts. The central courtyard is used in summer for occasional concerts and for outdoor film screenings – known as Cinema a la Fresca. Below ground level, reached by escalator, there is a supermarket. The Café Bar Mirador, with entrances both inside and outside the cloister, has a large sunny terrace with fantastic views over the harbour.

What the dispossessed Carmelites would have made of it all, we will never know, but they would probably have been happier with the **Museu Hernández Sanz Hernández Mora** (Mon, Wed–Sat 10am–1.30pm and 6–8pm, Sun 10am–1.30pm; free), which is also part of the complex. The museum displays the private collections of furniture, paintings, engravings and maps, dating from the 18th to the 20th centuries, which the Hernández family bequeathed to the city.

TWO CITY SQUARES

Some 50m/yds up the road to the east of the church and cloister you will come to the **Plaça de Miranda**, named after Almirante

Augusto Miranda y Godoy, who founded the naval station at Maó in 1916. A bust of the admiral tops a tall plinth in a commanding position above the harbour, but the square, albeit renovated, is still dominated by the ramp to an underground car park and the glass structures housing the pedestrian exits.

Back outside the cloister is the **Plaça d'Espanya**, a hub of constant coming and going. In the **Mercat del Peix**, the ornate fish market (mornings only), fish and seafood of all kinds are piled high on beds of ice. It is perched on a bastion that was part of the city wall – not the original medieval one, but the Renaissance structure that replaced it.

Reeling in the customers at the Mercat del Peix

THE HARBOUR

From here (or from the Portal de Mar running down the side of the Plaça de Sa Constitució), you will reach the gently curving road and broad steps of **Costa de Ses Voltes**, brightened by palm trees and flowering shrubs, that lead to the harbour spread out below. When cruise ships are in port, the area is busy with hair braiders, henna tattooists and stalls selling sandals, sunglasses and sarongs. Opposite Ses Voltes, glass-bottomed boats make hour-long trips round the harbour – an excellent way to get your bearings and gain a different perspective on the city.

Es Castell

The huge natural harbour is known simply as **Es Port E** and it is still a busy working port as well as a haven for pleasure craft, large and small, and some very luxurious. To the west of Ses Voltes, along the **Moll de Ponent** (meaning Western Quay) is the Zona Pesquera – the area used by the fishing fleet – and the Estació Marítima, the passenger terminal for ferries to mainland Spain and Mallorca. Opposite is a string of restaurants plus a couple of ceramic shops with some interesting pieces, shops selling the ubiquitous Menorcan sandals called *abarcas*, and the island's Pou Nou brand of T-shirts and casual cotton clothes. Past them, and past a splendid but neglected Art Nouveau-style building that was once the headquarters of the island electricity company, is the **Destileria Xoriguer** (Moll de Ponent 93; www.xoriguer.es), which distils and sells the island's gin and a number of brightly coloured herbal and fruit-based liqueurs. You can wander in and try some of the products, but the bottles on sale aren't much cheaper than you will find in other stores.

To the east of Ses Voltes, along the **Moll de Llevant** (Eastern Quay) is another line of restaurants with tables out on the pavement, ships' chandlers and a number of places that hire and repair boats. If you keep walking, you will come to Cala Figuera and a steep hill that leads up to the main Maó–Es Castell road.

ES CASTELL

From the main road, or from the terminal in Maó, buses run every half hour to **Es Castell ❷**, which is virtually a suburb of Maó. Built on a grid pattern by the British, it was first called

⊙ A TRIP ROUND THE HARBOUR

Taking a boat trip is the best way of appreciating the beauty of the city, which appears to rise straight out of the sea. Glass-bottomed boats, broadcasting a recorded commentary, run from the Ses Voltes area to the mouth of the harbour, where they stop so that passengers can have a look at the seabed from a viewing gallery. The boats go past the **Illa del Rei** (King's Island), where the British built a naval hospital that was used by the Spanish military until the 1960s. They also pass the **Illa Plana** (Flat Island), which was a quarantine site until the Lazareto station was built. You pass through the George Canal, constructed in 1900 to give easier access to steamships, and the forbidding walls of the ex-quarantine hospital on **Illa del Llazteret**. Between 1817 and 1917, some 400,000 people spent time here – some were detained for a quarantine period, while others were treated for a variety of infectious diseases, including yellow fever. Part of the building has been renovated and is now used as a conference centre and a summer holiday resort for social security workers. Ahead of you looms the impressive fortress of **La Mola**, and you can admire **Golden Farm** up on the hill to the north and the smart summer villas edging Cala Llonga. On the south side, you'll see boats at anchor in Cales Fonts and the colonial Collingwood House in Es Castell, which is now the **Hotel del Almirante**, before slipping back into harbour wiser than when you left.

Georgetown, and then became Villa Carlos, the name by which it is still known to many local people. The main square, the **Plaça de s'Esplanada** – once a parade ground, like the one of the same name in central Maó – is huge, but has a pleasant neighbourhood atmosphere in the early evening, when people gather at café tables in the centre, and children amuse themselves in a little play park. At one end of the square stands an imposing terracotta-coloured building that is now the police headquarters. It is shared by the offices of the Justice of the Peace and the local radio station, but they have to make do with small side entrances. At the other end of the square, huge cannons stand outside the **Museu Militar** (www.museo militarmenorca.com; June–Aug Mon–Fri and the first Sun of month 10am–1pm, Sept–May Mon, Wed, Fri and first Sun of the month 10am–1pm), home to an interesting collection of militaria.

A short walk from the square down Carrer Stuart brings you to **Cales Fonts**, a pretty harbour lined with fish restaurants that gets very animated at night.

If, instead of dropping down into Es Castell, you continue along the main road, you come to the turning for Sol d'Este, a development so named because this corner of Menorca is the eastern-most point, the place

Inside Fort de Marlborough

where the sun rises first in the morning. A number of bars and restaurants have names like The Rising Sun and El Sol Naciente. Nearby lie the ruins of the **Castell de Sant Felip** (www.museomilitarmenorca.com; June–Sept guided tour daily 10am, Oct–Nov and Mar–May Sat 10am; rest of the year by appointment only tel: 971 362 100).

A narrow road leads to **Cala Sant Esteve**, a pretty cove that relative inaccessibility and lack of a beach have enabled to retain its individuality. **Fort de Marlborough** (Apr–Nov daily 9.30am–4pm, Dec Thur–Sun 9.30am–3pm; last entry one hour before closing), an 18th-century British fort with a Martello tower and underground galleries, stages explosions as part of a 45-minute tour.

S'ALTRA BANDA

The road that runs from the west end of Maó's harbour will take you along the port's north side, which locally is called simply **S'Altra Banda** (The Other Side), past the naval base, towards a fine, terracotta manor house, officially called Finca Sant Antoni but usually known as **Golden Farm** (www.sanantoniomenorca.com). Legend has it that Admiral Horatio Nelson (1758–1805) used it not only as his headquarters but also for romantic trysts with his mistress, Lady Emma Hamilton. In fact, Lord Nelson made only one brief visit to Menorca – and Lady Emma did not come with him.

The road passes the smart suburb and little bay of **Cala Llonga**, before crossing a bleak, inhospitable stretch of land and a narrow causeway to the promontory on which stands the huge **Fortaleza de la Mola** (www.fortalesalamola.com; daily 10am–8pm; guided tours available, extra charge, for reservations tel: 971 364 040). The fort – also known as Fortaleza de Isabel II, after the Spanish queen – was built in the 1830s to replace the castle of Sant Felip, which the Spanish destroyed when they took the island in 1782, at the end of the second period of British occupation. It was highly fortified and given massive gun emplacements, but was never attacked. Your guide (if you have one) may or may not mention that, until as late as 1968, it served as one of Franco's most notorious political prisons.

THE NORTHEAST

The northeast of Menorca is a sparsely inhabited region, much of it protected by the Parc Natural de S'Albufera des Grau. Our route takes in the wetlands and dunes of the park and the village of Es Grau, as well as the remote headland and lighthouse of Favàritx. It then covers a couple of small developments, including Arenal d'en Castell – an example of what not to do when establishing a tourist resort. Next, it takes in the idyllic fishing port of Fornells and the bleak but beautiful Cap de Cavalleria with its fascinating birdlife, before either circling back via country roads to Fornells or returning to Maó along the main road.

If you are dependent on public transport, you will have to travel using buses from Maó to Es Grau, to Fornells and to Arenal d'en Castell, rather than making the circular trip.

S'ALBUFERA DES GRAU AND CAP DE FAVÀRITX

Take the road from Maó signposted to Fornells and after a very short distance turn off right towards Es Grau. The road runs through gently undulating land, with broad cycle tracks on either side, for about 4km (2.5 miles), before reaching the well-marked entrance to the **Parc Natural de S'Albufera** ❸ (www.balearsnatura.com; daily Apr–Sept 9am–6pm, Oct–Mar until

5pm; groups need a special permit – request at the reception centre, for details tel: 971 89 22 50; free). You can get information from the Centre de Recepción Rodríguez Femenias on the main Maó to Es Grau road, Km. 3.5 (http://balearsnatura.com; open year round 9am–4pm). There are plenty of clearly marked paths that make for easy walking through the protected land, where olives, juniper and prickly pears give way to Aleppo pines and strong, wiry marram grass as you approach the dunes surrounding the freshwater lake. Attracted by herons, terns, cormorants and ospreys, birdwatchers love this place, especially during spring and autumn migratory periods.

The lake is separated from the sea by a narrow strip of beach, which can also be reached by driving another 2km (1 mile) up the road from the park entrance to the unpretentious village of

The protected S'Albufera des Grau

A sombre event

In 1756 Favàritx was the setting for an ignominious incident in British history, when Admiral John Byng, sent to relieve British troops in Maó, became involved in a battle with the French and retreated, leaving the island in their hands. Back in England, he was court martialled for negligence and executed by firing squad.

Es Grau. Here, whitewashed houses cluster around the harbour and tamarisk grows with its roots almost in the sea. There are a couple of cafés and restaurants on the waterfront, and trips can be taken in summer on glass-bottomed boats out to little Illa d'en Colom and around the estuary.

Return to the main road and after approximately 7km (4 miles) take a right turn to **Cap de Favàritx ❹**, which is also part of the Parc Natural. This once rough and bumpy road has mostly been resurfaced and even given road markings. The landscape through which it runs is bleak and bare, with scant vegetation apart from scrub and succulents. It culminates in a grey slate headland lashed by the fierce Tramuntana wind, where the lighthouse, the **Far de Favàritx** (www.farsdebalears. org; visits upon previous arrangement tel: 971 363 066), shines out to sea. The cape has a beauty of its own and is the kind of place that makes you aware of the awesome power of nature.

NORTHERN RESORTS

Head back to the Fornells road now, and, if you are wondering what else this corner of the island holds, take a right turn after 7km (4 miles) towards **Port d'Addaia**. Turn right at the round-about to the port, which is pleasant enough but surrounded by a characterless sprawl of villas and apartments covering the headland between Cala d'Addaia and Cala Molins.

Return to the roundabout and head for **Na Macaret**, which is much nicer, although there's not much going on, and the beach is tiny. There's a pretty harbour, though, with fishermen's cottages clustered around, and ducks swimming on the tranquil waters. Two or three reasonably priced restaurants cater to tourists, some of whom come on the road train from Arenal d'en Castell. The housing development, mainly summer homes for people from Maó, is restrained and in keeping. In winter, everything closes down.

Back at the roundabout, the third exit leads to **Arenal d'en Castell**, the only place in the north of the island to have been given over completely to mass tourism. The resort is dominated by two huge, ugly hotels, with supermarkets and other facilities, resembling a rather ill-conceived public housing

The beach at sleepy Na Macaret

project. Behind them is a dense complex of holiday apartments. The beach, though – a wide horseshoe arc of golden sand surrounded by a wooden walkway illuminated at night – is splendid and the water is safe and shallow. Surfboards, pedaloes and sun loungers are available for hire. A snack bar on the beach promises live music nightly and there are more restaurants nearby.

Back to the main road now and head north. If you are looking for a quieter beach, turn off after 3km (1.5 miles) to **Son Parc**. Bordering an 18-hole golf course this is an up-market, although somewhat featureless, *urbanización*, its rows of holiday apartments and villas all remarkably similar. Its best feature – and the reason for its existence – is the lovely sandy beach, fringed by pinewoods.

Fornells is an idyllic fishing village with some great restaurants

SES SALINES AND FORNELLS

The 5km (3-mile) drive through shady pines between Son Parc and the Carretera Maó–Fornells is very pleasant. The main road then runs around the bay. Just before you get to Fornells, where a turning on the left is signed to Platjes de Fornells, the road leads through an elaborate arched gateway to a private 'country club' village. Almost opposite the turning is **Ses Salines**, an exclusive villa complex on the inlet, with a Club Náutic and attached restaurant, a small hotel (see page 138) and a strip of beach, usually busy with keen sailors and windsurfers. Windsurf Fornells gives lessons in sailing and water skiing as well as wind-surfing.

Follow the road along the sheltered inlet, and there's nowhere to go but **Fornells ❺**. This idyllically pretty fishing village is popular with the boating fraternity and with Catalan visitors from Barcelona. It has a number of pleasant hotels and makes a good base for exploring the coast. Fornells still has a working fishing fleet, even if tourism is more of a money spinner these days. A string of restaurants along the harbour sell the catch in various guises and all have their own version of *caldereta de llagosta*, the lobster stew that is Fornells' speciality (see page 101) and which King Juan Carlos has been known to order on several occasions, when the royal yacht drops anchor here. Prices are pretty kingly, too, but the stew is delicious. If it's beyond your budget, there are plenty of excellent, less expensive alternatives.

Fornells is a low-key place, bursting with civic pride, its pristine, whitewashed houses decked with gleaming dark-green shutters, narrow streets scented with flowering tobacco plants, and a modest, unadorned church, Sant Nicolau, with a bell tower.

Beyond the village you can either walk or drive to **Torre de Fornells** (daily 9.30am–4pm), a sturdy fortress built on the

Torre de Fornells

windy headland by the British in 1802. The defensive tower has been renovated, and there is a small museum inside concentrating on local and military history. Below the tower, a little shrine, the Ermita de Lourdes is surrounded by candles and flowers, both real and plastic. From this vantage point the headlands, buffeted by the Tramuntana, stretch out on either side of the bay, bleak and desolate.

CAP DE CAVALLERIA

From the crossroads about 3km (2 miles) back down the main road, there is a narrow road to **Cap de Cavalleria 6**. A short way along, a right turn is signposted to Cala Tirant, an attractive bay, but one that demands a rough and dusty 2km (1-mile) drive, or else a walk. Carry on towards Cap de Cavalleria, which was named after the estates into which Menorca was divided, for logistical purposes, after the Christian reconquest.

Continue driving for another 4km (2 miles) or so through wetlands alive with birds, and farmland where sheep and cattle graze, and you will come to a small car park, from where paths lead across hills and dunes to the beach.

Carry on driving, and you will come to the Roman settlement of Sanitja, discovered only in the 1980s. Archaeological digs are continuing, and further finds are being made. Three-week-long archaeological field schools are held here in the summer months. (See www.archaeology.institute for more information.)

You can drive to the lighthouse on the tip of the cape, passing the Roman site and the Torre de Sanitja, the Martello tower built by the British in 1798.

BINIMEL-LÀ AND CALA PREGONDA

Back down the road, the way you came, there is a turning to the beach of **Binimel-là**, a pretty place where a beach bar operates

◉ BIRDS ON THE CAPE

There is a wealth of birdlife on the drive to Cap de Cavalleria. Buzzards and herons are quite common and can be seen from the road; there are also two rare species, although these are less often seen. One is a type of vulture known as a moixeta (Neophron percnopterus); the other is the Balearic shearwater (Puffinus mauretanicus), belonging to the albatross family group. The shearwaters spend most of their lives at sea but come ashore from February to June to breed and lay their eggs in caves or holes in the ground. There are only about 3,000 reproductive pairs in the world, and only one chick from each clutch is raised. The birds leave for Cantabria and the English Channel, and return here in September.

in summer, and you can sometimes hire pedaloes. The last bit of the road is unmade and pretty rough, so it is advisable to leave the car in the carpark and walk the final stretch. If you want to swim at the secluded **Cala Pregonda** just round the coast to the west, you'll definitely have to walk, as there is no road. It's not a taxing walk; the path is unmarked, but as long as you follow the coast you should not go far wrong. It is a beautiful spot, its sandy beach backed by pine woods. Take a picnic, as there are no services or facilities here.

From the cape you can return to Fornells, if that is your base, by retracing your route past the Cavalleria turning. If you are heading back to Maó, continue on the rural road through farmland to Es Mercadal where you join the Me-1, the main highway.

Cala Pregonda

THE CENTRE OF THE ISLAND

The busy main road from Maó to Ciutadella is only 47km (30 miles) long, and, unless you get stuck behind a truck, the direct journey should take less than an hour. This route will make a number of stops, however, as well as offering the option of taking the old road, the Camí d'en Kane. Just outside Maó you can visit the prehistoric sites of Talatí de Dalt and Rafal Rubí before continuing to Alaior, a cheese-making centre, and to the pretty market town of Es Mercadal. Just outside the latter is Monte Toro, the highest point on the island and a major pilgrimage site. Ferreries is the next town on the main road, and a detour can be made from here to Santa Agueda, which is home to the remains of a castle and a Roman road. Just before reaching Ciutadella there are several more prehistoric sites that are worth visiting, in particular the great stone tomb called the Naveta d'es Tudons.

TALATÍ DE DALT AND RAFAL RUBÍ

Leaving Maó, you pass the monastery church of **Ermita de Gràcia** and the cemetery. The church was built in the late 15th century, and the nave is Gothic, but the striking snow-white facade dates from 1733. Inside, votive offerings give thanks from sailors and fishermen rescued from the seas.

Just 3km (2 miles) outside the capital, a sign points to the **Talatí de Dalt** ❼ (daily 10am–sunset; charge Apr–Oct). The settlement is believed to date from the end of the Bronze Age, *c.*1400BC. Surrounded by gnarled olive trees and carobs, this atmospheric site includes a large central *talayot*, some burial caves and the remains of several circular houses, but the star piece is a slim *taula* with a leaning column, believed to have come to rest by accident rather than design.

Back on the main road, you will soon see a sign for the **Navetes de Rafal Rubí**, an open site (free) with two collective ossuaries, stone structures shaped like upturned boats. Crawl through the low doorway of the better-restored one to appreciate the spacious interior, over 2m (6.5ft) high.

ALAIOR

The first town along the road is **Alaior 8** (pop. about 9,000), the third-largest on Menorca. Most of the cheese known as Queso de Mahón is made here, not in Maó. A mass of white houses cluster on a low hill, dominated by the sandstone church of **Santa Eulalia** (built 1674–90), with an exuberant Baroque doorway. There are several other impressive buildings, including Can Salort, in narrow Carrer Major, part of the

Alaior is dominated by its great sandstone church

Balearic Islands University. Opposite, the 18th-century Casas Consistoriales (another name for Town Hall) is splendid, especially its elaborate balcony and central staircase.

From the central Plaça del Constitució, Carrer Forn leads down to the former Franciscan **Convent de Sant Diego**, which functions as a cultural centre, exhibition gallery and a concert auditorium. Next door, the cloisters have been remodelled as an apartment block set around an attractive courtyard, the Pati de Sa Lluna – Courtyard of the Moon.

Carry on downhill (Carrer des Banyer) and you will reach **La Payesa** cheese factory, with a retail outlet opposite (www.la payesa.es; Mon–Fri 9am–1pm, 4–6pm). The factory itself cannot be visited. Coinga (www.coinga.com; Mon–Fri 9am–1.30pm and 4.30–8pm, Sat 10am–1pm), the other manufacturer, is on the edge of town in Carrer Es Mercadal.

CAMÍ D'EN KANE

The old **Camí d'en Kane**, the cross-island route built by the British in the early 18th century, leads past Alaior's cemetery, about 1.5km (1 mile) north of town. You can pick up the whole surviving stretch, from Maó to Es Mercadal, from a turning 2km (1 mile) along the road from Maó to Fornells. The narrow *camí* runs though gentle countryside, with dry-stone walls, some crumbling, some topped off with white-painted cement to keep them together. Every so often you pass one of the typical Menorcan olive-wood gates, and an occasional grand *finca*, but few crops are grown along the way, and the road is more interesting historically than scenically.

ES MERCADAL

If you are continuing west from Alaior on the main road, your next stop will be **Es Mercadal ⑨** (pop. 5,000), about 13km (8

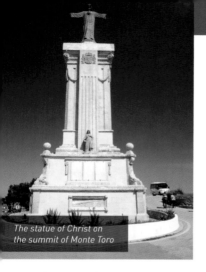

The statue of Christ on the summit of Monte Toro

miles) further on, and a good starting point for hikes through the surrounding countryside. Clustered at the foot of Monte Toro this is a sleepy old town of narrow streets and blindingly white houses, smothered with bougainvillaea blooms in summer. There's a pretty red-tiled *plaça* surrounding the **Església Paroquial de Sant Martin** (usually open for mass only), and stone bridges span the (mostly dry) river bed that skirts the town.

The lack of water in the stream makes it clear why one historical structure came to be built. The cistern, or *aljub*, was the brainwave of governor Richard Kane in 1733. Noting a connection between the shortage of water and frequent outbreaks of disease, he financed the project – a move that was more innovative than it sounds, at a time when the link between water, sanitation and health was little understood. The cistern, which holds 273,000 litres (54,600 gallons), works by collecting and storing the rain that falls on to a flat roof. From the road, all you can see is a narrow flight of steps up to a wooden gate that seems to lead nowhere.

The town's other claim to fame is that it plays host to several restaurants, specialising in authentic *cuina menorquina*. All are good, and one is excellent (see page 112). It is also worth visiting the **Centre Artesanal de Menorca** (Craft Centre;

Carrer Metge Camps; May–Oct Tue–Sat 10am–3pm, Mar–Apr until 2pm; free) located in the old military barracks, which date from 1904. Here you can learn about the past and present of Menorcan crafts and watch local artists at work.

MONTE TORO

At the eastern entrance to Es Mercadal is the clearly marked road to **Monte Toro** ❿. This is Menorca's highest point, at 358m (1,170ft); the road up is sinuous but excellent, and the view from the top is splendid.

There has been a shrine here since the 13th century when, according to legend, a bull led a group of monks to a statue of the virgin hidden in the rocks. As bull is *toro* in Spanish, it is easy to see how this story evolved, but the name most likely comes from the Arabic *al-tor*, meaning 'high place'. In the 17th century Augustinian monks built a sanctuary here and stayed till 1835, when monastic property was confiscated. Their church (daily 7am–7pm) was desecrated a century later during the Spanish Civil War, and most of what you see today, including the gaudy, Baroque-style altar, is the result of a 1940s renovation. The courtyard outside is a pleasant place, with a small

⊙ THE VERGE DEL MONTE TORO

The story above is not the only one connected to the statue of the Verge del Monte Toro. According to another local (more believable) tale, when the church was desecrated in 1936, a local man called Joan Albalat saved the figurine from the approaching flames and gave it to farmers at nearby Rafal des Frares to hide until the end of the Civil War. The container in which they buried it is displayed in a side chapel of the church.

A glistening altarpiece in the church of Sant Bartomeu

fountain and lots of glossy plants, and it's a popular spot for visitors to take photographs.

There is still a functioning convent here, and the nuns run the souvenir shop. It shares its hilltop home with the remains of a fort, built in anticipation of a Turkish invasion and a huge statue of Christ, commemorating those who died in an ill-advised Moroccan war in the 1920s, and is completely dwarfed by radar towers that are part of an army post.

In the café here you can get great sandwiches, which can be eaten on a sunny terrace, and there's a restaurant (www.sapo sadadeltoro.com) that does a reasonable *menú del dia*.

SA FARINERA AND FERRERIES

Sa Farinera (summer daily 10am–8pm; free), a converted manor house and mill just outside Ferreries, claims to be an ethnological museum and to sell local products, but is a bit of a let down. The children's playground and small go-kart track will please little ones, but most of the complex is just one huge souvenir shop, plus a restaurant.

The fifth-largest town on the island, **Ferreries** ⓫ (pop. 4,600), is also the highest, at 142m (465ft) above sea level, but is less picturesque than Alaior or Es Mercadal. The old centre, with narrow streets and the parish church of Sant Bartomeu, is attractive, but the town is dominated by streets of apartment blocks and an industrial area. However, this does mean that there is plenty of employment in Ferreries, mainly in the thriving shoe industry, so the town is prosperous and does not have to depend on tourism.

Since it is so well situated for walks through the hills to the north and the lush ravines of the south, the town is increasingly geared up to *turisme rural*. On Saturday morning farm produce and craft items are sold in a large market in the modern Plaça d'Espanya.

PUIG DE SANTA AGUEDA

About 3km (1.5 miles) west of Ferreries is the turning to Binisues and **Puig de Santa Agueda** (264m/866ft), the third-highest peak on the island. A sprawling 18th-century manor house contains the **Museu de Ciències Naturals de Menorca** (Tue–Sun 10.30am–7pm, rest of the year by appointment only tel: 971 373 728), which not only presents Menorca's rich biodiversity, but also reproduces interiors of a typical manor house. It's about an hour's walk from Binisues up a steep path through a grove of cork oak to a remarkably well-preserved section of Roman path. On the summit are the ruins of the Castell de Santa Agueda, a fort dating from the Moorish period. There isn't much left, but the view is spectacular.

TALAYOTS AND *TAULES*

Back along the main road to Ciutadella, near the Km 37 sign, just after you pass a strange mock castle on your

Barraques

You may notice pyramids in the fields as you drive along the Ciutadella road, but these are not ancient structures. Local farmers have put to good use some of the many stones that litter their fields, and built livestock shelters, known as *barraques*.

right (Castillo Menorca, a shopping centre with children's playground), there is an inconspicuous pink sign for Torrellafuda on the left. About 1km (0.5 mile) down a bumpy lane you come to the well-preserved *talayot* and *taula* of **Torrellafuda** (open site; free), beautifully set in a copse of holm oaks.

Although the lovely settlement of **Torre Trencada** ⑫ (Apr–mid-Nov daily 8am–9pm, rest of the year until 6pm; free) is just 1km (0.5 mile) away as the crow flies, to reach it you have to return to the main road, then turn left 2km (1 mile) further on. At first the road is asphalted, but when you reach the Camí Vell it becomes rough and potholed, running between crumbling dry-stone walls (go left at the fork). A five-minute walk through farmland from the car park brings you to an outstanding *taula*, which, unusually, is supported by two other pillars rather than one. The walls surrounding the settlement have all but disappeared, but there is a *talayot* and several burial caves, which are thought to be medieval rather than prehistoric. The site is popular, and people often come here to picnic among the trees. Nearby, in an abandoned quarry, S'Hostal (www.lithica. es; Mon–Sat 9.30am–2.30pm, 4.30pm–sunset, Sun 9.30am–2.30pm) is a stone labyrinth and sculpture garden.

NAVETA D'ES TUDONS

About 1km (0.5 mile) along the main road, the **Naveta d'es Tudons** ⑬ (year-round Mon 9.30am–4.30pm, Tue–Sun 9am–8pm; free on Mon and Nov–Mar) is clearly signed, with a left filter and a large car park, for this Bronze Age burial chamber is one of the most famous prehistoric monuments in Menorca. It stands alone in the middle of a field and has a magical atmosphere – as long as you don't arrive at the same time as a tour bus on a flying visit. During excavations in the 1950s, the remains of about 100 people were discovered in this two-storey

The golden walls of Ciutadella rise above the harbour

ossuary, along with personal effects of bone and bronze. The boat-shaped *naveta* is believed to be the oldest roofed building in Europe.

CIUTADELLA

Menorca's second city, **Ciutadella** ⓮ has elegant manorial houses, grand churches, narrow cobbled streets and a friendly, lived-in atmosphere. As Medina Minurka it was the Moorish capital of the island, and, when Alfonso III of Aragón entered the city in 1287, it became the Christian capital. A Turkish army destroyed most of the town in 1558, following a 10-day siege. It was rebuilt, but in 1722 the British gave the status of capital to Maó, because Ciutadella's narrow inlet simply could not compete with Maó's harbour. However, in terms of its natural beauty and choice seafood restaurants, Es Port is hard to beat today.

Although Ciutadella means Little City it has a population of 28,000, only slightly lower than that of Maó. As well as exploring the town and port, this route takes a trip to the northwest corner of the island, to the lovely bay and ancient caves of Cala Morell and the beach at Algaiarens. Buses run three times a day from Plaça dels Pins, but a car obviously gives you more flexibility.

THE HARBOUR

Ciutadella's harbour, **Es Port Ⓐ**, is a delight – the archetypal Mediterranean harbour. If you arrive by sea, you will be bowled over by the setting: the ochre-coloured city walls and the fortified structure of the former town hall rising behind them. The long narrow inlet is full of yachts, easily outnumbering the fishing boats, and the quays are lined with cafés and restaurants whose tables reach almost to the water's edge.

You can walk along the Camí de Baix (Lower Road) then take steps up to **Passeig de Sant Nicolau**, which runs past the Club

⊙ THE USEFUL SIDE OF THE HARBOUR

The far side of Ciutadella's harbour, connected by a pedestrian bridge, is less busy and interesting than the near one, but it offers a number of useful services. It is here that you can purchase tickets for the car and passenger ferries to Mallorca, and where you will disembark if you arrive by sea. Boat trips to Platja de Son Saura and Cala en Turqueta on the south coast also start here. As well as a couple of restaurants with excellent harbour views, there are the offices of car-hire companies, and outlets that rent boats and jet skis and organise fishing trips. Further along the quay are busy boat yards, where the activity reminds us that Ciutadella is still a working port.

Náutic and gives views of elegant summer homes set in gardens on the far side. Continue to the **Castell de Sant Nicolau** (Tue–Sat 10am–1pm, 6–8pm; free), a sturdy octagonal tower with a small, rather uninspiring museum inside. This is, however, a great place from which to watch the sunset. Outside, a bust commemorates David Glasgow Farragut (1801–70), the son of a local man who immigrated to the US.

The old Ajuntament building in the Plaça d'es Born

Farragut became the first four-star admiral of the US and was given a hero's welcome when he visited Ciutadella in 1867.

At the tower, the broad, palm-lined promenade changes its name to Passeig Marítim and continues round the headland as far as little Cala des Degollador, where the road to the southern resorts begins at a roundabout.

PLAÇA D'ES BORN

Back on the quayside, the sloping Baixada Caplonc leads up past souvenir stalls and shops to the ceremonial square, **Plaça d'es Born B**, its grandeur somewhat marred by a plethora of parked cars. The square is dominated in the centre by a large obelisk commemorating those who died defending the town against the Turks in 1558. A market is held here on Friday and Saturday (9am–2pm), and on 23–24 June it is the main site of the Festa de Sant Joan (see page 96), when horsemen ride among the crowds, their steeds prancing and circling on their hind legs.

Most of the buildings in the square date from the early 19th century. Dominating the west end is the grand, crenellated Town Hall – or the Ajuntament – with a colourful mosaic on the ground outside. It houses the main tourist office (Mon 9.30am–2pm, Tue–Sun 9am–8pm). The sounds emanating from a primary school in the building next door typify Ciutadella's pleasing mix of historical and modern, majestic and mundane. Along the north side, the Teatre Principal, restored after years of neglect, serves as both theatre and cinema. Next door is the Cercle Artístic, an artists' association; its café has good harbour views from the back.

In the southeast corner, beside the post office, stands the great bulk of the **Església Sant Francesc** (open only for mass; weekdays 7.30pm, Sat 4.30 and 7.30pm, Sun 9.30 and 11am, and 7.30pm). It is a mixture of styles as it originated in the late 13th century, was burned by the Turks in 1558, rebuilt, augmented in the 18th and 19th centuries and desecrated in the Civil War.

The east side of the square is lined with elegant, but somewhat run-down, mansions, built for aristocratic families whose descendants, mostly based in Barcelona or Madrid, come for visits in summer. The ground floors have been converted into cafés and souvenir shops. The **Palau de Torre Saura** has a splendid portal, a magnificent inner courtyard and Renaissance-style putti on the roof. The noble facade of the Palau Vivó is decorated with oriel windows and balconies, and the atrium contains a magnificent double staircase.

PALAU DE CAN SALORT

The only one of these grand palaces that can be visited (apart from the Palau Saura which is now an exhibition space) is the neoclassical **Palau de Can Salort** ⓒ (Mon–Sat 10am–2pm;

The Palau de Torre Saura

entrance via the side door in Carrer Major del Born). Built in 1600 for the Salort family, it was purchased by Pedro Martorell y Olives, who redesigned it in 1813, modelling its facade on that of La Llotja, the Barcelona Stock Exchange. It is well worth a visit. You buy your ticket in the courtyard from a kiosk that resembles a Punch and Judy stall, before exploring the rooms: a kitchen with a vast tiled stove running almost the length of one wall; the children's bedroom, with a cradle and a pram; a well-stocked library; a salon with family portraits; and a dining room, with a table laid for dinner. In the inner patio you'll find the first bar authorised to operate within the protected historic building, Moriarty.

PLAÇA DE LA CATEDRAL
Carrer Major del Born leads to the **Plaça de la Catedral**, where street entertainers amuse the crowds and a tourist office (see page 132) is housed in the imposing Consell Insular building

opposite the **Catedral de Santa María**  (May–Oct Mon–Sat 10am–4pm). Built of honey-coloured sandstone, it was begun in the early 14th century on the site of an earlier mosque but desecrated by the Turks in 1558. It was damaged by fire during the following century, but was well renovated and in 1795 was elevated to the status of a cathedral, when a papal edict restored the bishopric of Menorca (there had been one back in the 5th century).

The main facade and splendid doorway are in the 19th-century neoclassical style, but the broad nave is Catalan Gothic, as is the great marble altar, covered by an ornate *baldachino*. The Port de la Llum (Door of Light), damaged in the Civil War and subsequently restored, retains its 14th-century ornamentation – magnificent, fabled creatures and coats of arms. Organ concerts (small fee) are held throughout the summer, providing a good opportunity not only to listen to the soaring music but also to appreciate the effects of the light filtering through the stained-glass windows.

The quiet inner courtyard of the 18th-century **Palau Episcopal** (Mon–Sat 9am–4pm; free) in the Carrer de Cal Bisbe connects the palace and the cathedral. The rest of the palace is closed to the public.

Catedral de Santa María

CHURCHES AND MANSIONS

If you take the narrow Carrer del Roser opposite the main door of the cathedral, you will come to the intricate and beautiful doorway of the 17th-century **Es Roser** (http://balearscultural tour.net; May–Oct Mon–Sat 11am–1.30pm and 6–9pm; Nov–Apr 10.30am–1pm and 5.30–8pm; free). Once a parish church, it has had many uses since its desecration in the Civil War. Now renovated by the town council, it serves as an exhibition centre. Its light, airy central hall, the Sala Municipal, hosts temporary exhibitions of modern art.

Just around the corner, next to La Guitarra restaurant (see page 109) is another historic building that has become a venue for art and photographic exhibitions: the **Palau Saura Morel** **E** (Espacio de Arte Xec Coll; exhibitions Mon–Fri 10.30am–2pm, 6–9pm, Sat 10.30am–2pm; free), whose renovation was also largely funded by the town council. The exterior of the palace looks particularly lovely at night, when the overhanging eaves and the arches of the upper storey are illuminated, and the light picks out the intricate details. Many of the buildings in Ciutadella's old town are lit at night, or else gently illuminated by the old-fashioned street lamps; they glow like gold in the narrow streets that fall quiet when visitors return to the resorts at the end of a day's visit.

RESTORING THE PAST

Continuing to the left along Carrer del Santissím and into Carrer des Seminari, you reach the 17th-century **Convent i Església de San Agustin El Socors**, originally an Augustinian monastery. Most of the building is closed to the public, but summer concerts are held in the pretty cloister, planted with lemon trees, and the ground floor houses the **Museu Diocesà** (summer Tue–Sat 10.30am–1.30pm and 6–9pm,

Fish stall at the market

Sun mornings free, winter Tue–Sat 10.30am–1.30pm). As well as ecclesiastical items, its displays include interesting archaeological finds and a collection of landscape paintings by Pere Daura (1896–1976), who was born in Ciutadella.

On the next corner stands the baronial **Can Saura**. It is the main seat of Ciutadella's courts. At the back of the building is a centre for the elderly. Also in Carrer des Seminari, on the corner of Carrer Sant Crist, is **Església de Sant Crist** (daily 9am–1pm, 5–9pm; free), built in 1661. Above the altar of this tiny, simple church is a powerful crucifixion figure, restored in 2006, which is deeply venerated because drops of perspiration are said to have appeared on it in the late 17th century.

THE MARKET AND SES VOLTES

Now make a detour down Carrer Sant Crist and turn right towards Plaça Françesc Netto and the adjoining Plaça de la Libertat, an attractive arcaded square where the **Mercat** (market) is held on Tuesday to Saturday mornings. Mountains of fruit, vegetables and meat are on sale in the green-and-white-tiled market hall, while fish is available from numerous stalls in the 19th-century pavilion. Bars around the squares do a brisk trade when the market is open.

Retrace your steps to the corner of Carrer des Seminari, and you emerge into a *plaça* and a street that is officially called Carrer de Josep Maria Quadrado, but is always known simply as **Ses Voltes** . Café tables are set out in the centre of the square, which is framed by whitewashed arches, and the shady arcades continue up the street, where, among the gift shops, there is an appetising *confitería* (pastry shop) selling huge *ensaimadas*, and a shoe shop specialising in stylish *abarcas* (see page 91).

PLAÇA NOVA AND PLAÇA DE SES PALMERES

The road ends in another attractive square full of café tables, **Plaça Nova**. Here the busy, pedestrianised shopping street of Camí de Maó runs to Plaça Alfons III, widely known as **Plaça de Ses Palmeres** (Square of the Palm Trees). This is the eastern

Relaxing at the Plaça de Ses Palmeres

edge of town and it marks the spot where the road from Maó reached the old city gates. Traffic roars along the Avinguda de la Constitució on the far side but the square itself has been paved and pedestrianised, brightened with flowers and lined on two sides by cafés and restaurants.

The white windmill on the other side of the avenue is the **Molí d'es Comtes**, built in the late 18th century and one of the few windmills still standing on the island. There is a bar and shop on the ground floor, and an adjoining restaurant serves good grilled meats (www.asador-molidescomte.com).

THE BASTIÓ DE SA FONT

Go back to Ses Voltes now and take a right turn down Carrer de Santa Clara. You will pass the Monestir de Santa Clara.

Bronze Age and Roman items in the Museu Municipal

Continue straight along the narrow road ahead and you reach the stocky **Bastió de Sa Font** Ⓖ, a great bastion built in the late 17th century as part of Ciutadella's fortifications. It now houses the **Museu Municipal** (Tue–Sat 10am–2pm, 6–9pm, free on Wed). The vaulted galleries of this excellent museum

> ### Early surgery
>
> Some of the skulls in the Museu Municipal show signs of trepanning, a gruesome method used in cranial surgery. Remarkably, some show wounds that have healed, proving that the patients must have survived.

house Bronze Age skulls, weapons and domestic utensils from the *talayotic* period and Roman coins, jewellery and oil lamps, all of which are very well displayed (though most of the information is in Catalan, there is a small leaflet in other languages available). Some of the finds come from the caves at Cala Morell.

COMPLETING THE TOUR

Walk back along Carrer de sa Muradela, overlooking a dry river bed where little flower and vegetable gardens have been cultivated, and you will soon be back at the harbour and Plaça des Born, having almost completed a tour of the city. Not far from here, on Carrer Sant Rafel (at No. 11), is the house where painter José Roberto Torrent Prats lived. Known as 'the Menorcan Van Gogh', Torrent was born in Ciutadella in 1904. Unlike many provincial artists, who head for the cultural centres of Europe, Torrent spent his life here.

If you are catching a bus from Ciutadella to your next destination, cross Plaça des Born to Plaça de s'Esplanada, also known as Plaça des Pins after the pine trees dotted around the shady square. There are kiosks selling sweets, cafés with outdoor tables, and a children's playground. It has a nice, neighbourly feel to it, especially in the evening, when you are likely to see more local people than tourists.

CALA MORELL AND PLATJES D'ALGAIARENS

Just to the north of Ciutadella lies a cluster of tourist resorts, with all the usual facilities, and where most of the accommodation is block-booked by tour companies; these include Cala en Blanes, Cala en Forcat and Los Delfinos. The two most interesting places are Cala Morell and Platjes d'Algaiarens.

Cala Morell ⓰, some 9km (5.5 miles) from Ciutadella, is one of the few places on the northwest coast where development has been permitted – and this only because it was largely done before the more stringent laws came into effect. It is a very upmarket development, however, with gleaming white villas set in spacious gardens, surrounded by pines, and a network of broad, well-lit roads.

Cala Morell

As you enter the complex, take the left turn at the roundabout with a model *talayot* in the centre. This leads both to a pebbly beach, set in a stunning cove and popular with snorkellers, and a complex of 14 Bronze and Iron Age caves, the **Necrópolis de Cala Morell** (open site; free). Set in the rocks right beside the road, the caves are extraordinary, with niches, chimneys and wall carvings, and their roofs supported by central pillars. It is believed that the caves were used as dwellings as well as for tombs, or ossuaries.

Go back the way you came and after about 3km (2 miles) a signed-posted road leads through farmland and some beautiful pinewoods to the fine, sandy **Platjes d'Algaiarens**, where twin beaches (Platja des Tancats and Platja des Bot) are set in a horseshoe-shaped bay. The bays and beaches are all privately owned and, in summer, to keep numbers down, a guardian at the gate will collect a charge for driving down the final 1km (0.5 mile). However, it's a very beautiful spot and well worth the fee if you want to spend a couple of hours or more here. You are welcome to walk down without paying.

THE SOUTH OF THE ISLAND

This route runs from Ciutadella to Maó, taking in the major resorts and beaches of Cala Santa Galdana, Son Bou and Cala N'Porter and a number of lovely little coves, some accessible only on foot or by rough tracks (just accessible by car). It includes the fertile Barranc d'Algendar; Son Catlar and Torre d'en Gaumés, the two best-preserved prehistoric settlements on the island; and the sleepy town of Es Migjorn Gran. To the southeast are the funerary caves of Cales Coves; the architect-designed 'fishermen's village' of Binibeca Vell; and Sant Lluís, a small town founded by the French. The distance would be small if there were a coast road, but you have to keep returning to the Me-1. However, these detours involve some attractive drives and the opportunity to make discoveries en route.

THE SOUTHWEST CORNER

Leaving Ciutadella from the roundabout at the end of the Passeig Marítim, a road runs straight down the coast, linking a number

Son Catlar: the largest ancient settlement in the Balearics

of somewhat featureless, sprawling resorts. The best of them is **Cala Blanca** (about 4km/2.5 miles from the city) with pine-lined streets and a small sandy beach, although the huge Hotel Globales Mediterrani that looms up as you approach is rather off-putting. Another 5km (3 miles) through flat, rocky terrain brings you to the island's southwest point, **Cap d'Artruix**. Apart from the lighthouse and a line of rather drab villas, there's little to see, but visitors on hired bikes can take full advantage of the flat terrain, and a small road train links the windy cape with the nearby resorts. The nicest of these are **Son Xoriguer** and **Cala en Bosc** – the latter has an attractive marina and is very popular with the boating crowd as well as with families.

SON CATLAR

Back to Ciutadella now, where you should take a right turn at the roundabout on to a road signposted to Sant Joan de

Missa and Cala en Turqueta and marked Camí Rural. Rural it certainly is, and you may be surprised, so close to the city centre, to see chickens wandering in the road. When you reach the Son Vivó farmhouse – an imposing building– take the right fork down a narrow, potholed road for about 5km (3 miles) to **Son Catlar** ⑯ (daily; free), one of Menorca's most important monuments.

Still enclosed by its original, 1km (0.5-mile) long perimeter wall, Son Catlar is the largest preserved settlement in the Balearic Islands. Established c.1400BC, it probably reached its heyday around the 3rd century BC, and was abandoned at the end of the Roman period. There is a splendid doorway in the wall, and within the enclosed area five *talayots* and a *taula* can easily be seen. One of the special features of the site is the *hypogaeum*, a small underground chamber that was used for funerary purposes. There is a large car park, an information kiosk and public toilets. Take insect repellent, as flies can sometimes be an irritation.

SANT JOAN AND CALA EN TURQUETA

Go back to the Son Vivó fork now, and it's around 2km (1 mile) down a bumpy road to the **Ermita de Sant Joan de Missa** (Mon 4–6pm; free), a compact, whitewashed chapel, festooned with vines and with a double-bell wall. It's a peaceful, pretty place but, owing to the limited opening times, most people only see it from the outside. Beyond the chapel to the left, a track branches off to the left towards Cala Macarella, but it's in extremely poor condition. If you want to visit Macarella beach, it's better to go to Cala Santa Galdana and walk along the clifftop.

Take the right fork, instead, signed to **Cala en Turqueta** ⑰, and after a short distance you come to another right turn,

Cala en Turqueta is popular, despite being hard to access

with a 'Welcome' sign and a kiosk where a caretaker ensures that no more than 120 cars take the rough and rocky track down to the car park. You could walk down – it's only about 1.5km (1 mile) – although passing cars throw up quite a lot of dust. It's a lovely cove with clear turquoise waters and walks over the headland through pines and juniper bushes. If you are lucky, you may see a brightly coloured hoopoe, or hear its distinctive call. There are few facilities at the beach, but ice creams and cold drinks are on sale in summer, and there are rudimentary portaloos.

CALA SANTA GALDANA

Back to the main Me-1 now and, after approximately 16km (10 miles), just before you reach Ferreries, take the turning to **Cala Santa Galdana** 🔞. This is a good, well-surfaced road, passing neat, white-painted cottages and well-tended vegetable gardens, which soon give way to fragrant pine woods. On the 7km (4-mile) drive you also pass two equestrian centres advertising evening shows, and the S'Atalaia camping site (see page 117).

Cala Santa Galdana is a salutary example of tourist development let loose on a perfect spot. Pine-studded cliffs drop down to a sheltered bay with sparkling waters and sand so white that it looks almost unreal. As if this wasn't enough, the **Barranc d'Algendar** cuts through the cliffs here, its stream widening out into a broad, rush-lined river as it reaches the sea.

Back in the early 1970s, this spot proved irresistible, and the developers moved in. Now, three large hotels dominate the small bay, and the Passeig Marítim, paralleling the river, is lined with restaurants and pizzerias, where tomato ketchup on the tables comes as standard. But let's not be churlish: the resort has everything you could ask for in terms of an active holiday – biking, hiking and pony trekking, as well as diving and fishing. It caters well for families, too; the waters are safe and shallow and there's a well-equipped children's playground right in the town centre.

As you drive in, over a narrow bridge, there is a large car park on your right; if it's full, as it may well be in high summer, you shouldn't have to drive far along the Passeig Marítim to find a space. From here you can wander along the commercial strip, past the villas that are part of the Hotel Cala Galdana complex, and the boats bobbing in the marina, where the mouth of the river separates the main resort from the beach. There's a narrow pedestrian bridge across it, which leads to the Restaurant El Mirador, set on a little promontory. The views are absolutely gorgeous, so it's worth stopping for a drink, but the food is only average for its price and service does not always come with a smile.

CALA MACARELLA AND CALA MITJANA

Another advantage of Cala Santa Galdana is that there are two lovely little beaches in unspoiled coves within easy walking distance, and one a little further afield. From the road beside Hotel Audax (wooden steps lead from the back of a small car park) you can walk through pine woods to **Cala Macarella** in about 30 to 40 minutes. Lack of vehicle access helps keep numbers down in this lovely little bay, flanked by cliffs, but it is far from deserted. The sand is fine, the water clear, and a small bar provides refreshments and shower facilities in summer.

If you feel up to a somewhat longer walk, tiny **Cala Macarelleta**, around the next headland, is more secluded, and therefore popular with nude sunbathers.

From the other side of Cala Santa Galdana, behind the monolithic Hotel Sol Gavilanes (and another car park) a path leads

◎ BARRANC D'ALGENDAR

The Barranc d'Algendar runs for about 6km (4 miles) from just west of Ferreries to Cala Santa Galdana. It's the most dramatic and probably the most beautiful of Menorca's limestone gorges. The vegetation is varied, ranging from pines and fruit trees to lush, almost subtropical foliage, while thick reeds and rushes border the river at the Santa Galdana end – unusually, the stream through the gorge runs with water all year round. Butterflies follow you on your way and a wealth of birdlife includes buzzards, kestrels and kites. An individual walker will be faced with a moral decision when reaching gates marked 'Propiedad Privada' (Private Property), but access problems are smoothed out if you go on an organised hike, which can be arranged in Cala Santa Galdana (see page 86).

Farmhouse near Es Migjorn Gran

through stone-scattered woodland, redolent with the smell of pines, to **Cala Mitjana**, an idyllic little cove with crystal-clear waters and huge caves in the cliffs. There are no facilities here, so bring supplies if you are coming for the day; the easy walk takes less than 20 minutes, so it is not far to carry a picnic and a beach mat.

If you continue along the road behind the Sol Gavilanes, through quiet streets lined with smart villas set in colourful flowery gardens, you will find a number of places marked 'Mirador', where viewing platforms give stupendous views over the bay.

ES MIGJORN GRAN, SANT TOMÀS AND SON BOU

Head back to Ferreries now, and turn right just before you enter the town. The curvy road runs 6km (4 miles) through the lush, fertile landscape, limestone rock faces and well-cultivated terraces to **Es Migjorn Gran** ⑲. This sleepy town, built by the

The beach at Son Bou

Spanish in the 18th century, has a meandering Carrer Major, lined with spick-and-span, dark-shuttered houses. There is not much here to detain you but, as well as being the starting point for an energetic walk down the Barranc de Binigaus to the sea (about 5km/3 miles each way), it also has one of the best restaurants on the island, **S'Engolidor** (see page 113).

It's only about 5km (3 miles) down the road from the town to **Sant Tomàs**, a pleasant but undistinguished resort that originally grew up here because the beaches were long, broad and splendid. They have been helped by a bit of artifice in recent years, however: in 1989 a freak storm made off with all the sand and the crisp white powder you walk through today had to be imported.

The beaches of Sant Tomàs almost meet up with those of the next resort, **Son Bou** 20. You can walk along, but to reach it by road you have to go back to the main road. You enter Son Bou through a dramatic arch in the rocks and immediately ahead, where you should have a view of the sea, is the bulk of the huge Hotel Sol Pinguinos Milanos. The resort is a sprawling one, but the pristine dunes and beach are now under a protection order (like much of the coast). No more development along the water's edge has been permitted and other buildings here have been limited to four storeys. A couple of inoffensive snack bars cater to visitors, and pedaloes and sun loungers are for hire. A little road train takes visitors from their hotels down to the beach.

If you walk to the left, past the Sol Pinguinos Milanos on one side of the road and ranks of apartments on the other, you will reach the remains of the 5th-century **Basílica Paleocristiana** which was not discovered until 1951. The entrance gate is usually shut but there is a good view of the beach-side settlement from over a low boundary wall.

TALAYOTIC SITES

On your way back to the main road at Alaior, take a right turn down a well-surfaced road to **Torre d'en Gaumés** ㉑ (Wed–Sat 10am–8pm, Tue and Sun 9am–4pm; free on Mon), which is the second largest of Menorca's prehistoric settlements. Believed to date in part from the pre-*talayotic* era, it has three *talayots*, a *taula*, circular dwellings, a hypostyle (the name for a hall with supporting columns),

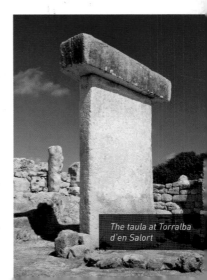

The taula at Torralba d'en Salort

Local legend

According to legend a Moor named Xoroi took refuge in the Cova d'en Xoroi after the reconquest. He eventually abducted a local farmer's daughter and fathered three sons by her. When his hiding place was discovered, Xoroi jumped into the sea and the girl and her children lived (we are told) happily ever after.

and caves and cisterns carved out of the soft sandstone rock.

Yet another megalithic site, one that includes the most beautiful *taula* of all, is reached via the minor road from Alaior to Cala N'Porter. Excavations began in 1973 on **Torralba d'en Salort** ㉒ (Sun–Mon 10am–1pm, Wed 10am–5pm, Tue and Thu–Sat 10am–8pm), but there are still more discoveries to be made. A small bronze statue of a calf was found here (now in the Museu de Menorca), indicating that the bull was worshipped in Menorca as it was in the rest of the Mediterranean.

CALA N'PORTER AND CALES COVES

Cala N'Porter does not have a great deal of character. The sandy beach is pleasant enough, surrounded by high cliffs, with tall grasses growing where the deep gorge meets the sea, and the waves can be good for surfing, but to reach the sprawling development above you have to climb up a long flight of steps cut into the limestone, or go some distance up a hill. This means that the road train has to work overtime, ferrying people back and forth to their hotels.

The most popular attraction here is the **Cova d'en Xoroi** ㉓ (www.covadenxoroi.com; daily June–Sept 11am–sunset, Oct 3pm–sunset), a large cave set in the sheer cliff face some 25m (80ft) above the sea and sky. Although you can't explore the cave itself and the fee is a little steep, the views and the little café terrace are glorious. At night the cave is transformed into a disco, which opens at 11pm and keeps going (loudly) until the early hours.

Just for once, you don't have to go back to the main road. Instead, head towards **Sant Climent** (best known for its jazz club, see page 95), where there is a substantial English expatriate population. You could make a detour to the development of Son Vitamina, from where you can walk to the impressive **Cales Coves** ㉔. This is the most important *talayotic* necropolis on the island and one that was still used, for ritual rather than burial purposes, by the Romans. They are put to good use today, as well, by young backpackers who sleep rough in them during the summer, despite occasional attempts by the authorities to keep them away.

Cales Coves was a necropolis but has since had various uses

BINIBECA VELL AND ITS NEIGHBOURS

From Sant Climent, take the excellent road in the direction of Binidalí, parallel with the airport runway. It heralds the beginning of 'the Binis'– the rash of *urbanizaciones* with the Bini prefix (an Arabic legacy) that cover this part of the coast, linked by roads that often lead, frustratingly, to dead ends. There are some nice beaches here, usually accessible only on foot, but the developments are all pretty soulless and similar, until you get to **Binibeca Vell** ㉕ (also spelled Binibequer Vell).

The houses in this architect-designed 'fishermen's village' – Poblat de Pescadors – washed in brilliant white, look as if they are made of icing sugar. Stairs, chimneys and balconies are all totally harmonious. Narrow, winding alleys emerge into interior courtyards, finished with natural stone and decorated with ceramic tiles; there are palms and orange trees at every corner; and bougainvillaea tumbles over garden walls. Bars and restaurants, a market place, a church and quay have also been constructed as integral parts of the settlement. The vast majority of the apartments and villas are either holiday accommodation or summer homes for people from mainland Spain.

The overall effect is beautiful, but strangely unreal, and the hordes

Architect-designed Binibeca Vell

of visitors dropped off by tour coaches during the summer months for a quick tour of the village only add to the impression that this is part of a film set. Those old enough to remember the cult 1960s UK television series *The Prisoner* may expect a large balloon to follow them around, blocking their escape from the village.

SANT LLUÍS AND CALA D'ALCAUFAR

Now head about 6km (4 miles) inland to **Sant Lluís** ㉖, a friendly town built on a grid pattern by the French during their brief period of occupancy (1756–63). There is a car park by the ornate, dove-capped roundabout as you enter town. Halfway up the main road, the neoclassical parish church stands on one side of the road, while the Ajuntament (town hall) is in a small square on the other.

Situated at the far end of town is the **Molí de Dalt** (Mon–Sat 10am–1pm), a lovingly restored windmill that houses a small ethnological museum with a collection of traditional farm tools and milling equipment.

If you have some time to spare on your way back to Maó you could stop off at one final, and very impressive, megalithic site, **Trepucó** (free access), just off the main road. If you prefer a last drink by the sea, there is a string of beach-side developments around the southeastern tip of the island. **Cala d'Alcaufar** is perhaps the nicest, as it has retained some of the atmosphere of the fishing village it always was, long before the tourists arrived. The waterfront is lined with low white buildings and boathouses with brightly painted doors, and fishermen go about their business while visitors sip drinks at café tables, or soak up the sun. From here, or from Sant Lluís, it is just a few kilometres back to the centre of Maó, or to the airport, and your journey's end.

Menorca is an ideal place for
watersports pros and beginners

WHAT TO DO

OUTDOOR ACTIVITIES

Most outdoor activities in Menorca are those you do on, in or under the water, including diving, sailing, wind and kitesurfing, water-skiing, fishing and, of course, swimming. However, the island is also a great place for walking and bird watching, and thousands of visitors come here for those reasons, especially in the spring and autumn, when the mild weather makes walking a pleasure, and numerous species of migrating birds delight birdwatchers. Cycling is a good way of seeing parts of the island that are not readily accessible by road, and much of the terrain is relatively flat and undemanding. And as a consequence of the islanders' love of horses, Menorca is also a good place for riding.

WINDSURFING AND SAILING

The winds and waves of Menorca are ideal for windsurfing and sailing, and there are numerous places where you can take lessons, rent equipment or just spend your whole day enjoying the water. On the northeast coast, Fornells is the main centre of activity. **Windsurf Fornells** (tel: 664 335 801, www.windfornells.com) offers windsurfing, sailing and water-skiing. The safe, shallow waters here make it a particularly good place for beginners. To the west, **Surf & Sail** in Son Xoriguer (tel: 971 387 105 or mobile 629 749 944, www.surfsailmenorca.com) organises all kinds of activities for all abilities. And in the southeast corner, **SUPaire** (tel: 619 573 211, www.supaire.com), offers kayaking, paddle-boarding and windsurfing.

Snorkelling in Menorca's crystal-clear waters

DIVING

Diving in Menorca's sparkling waters can be an unforgettable experience, and there are many outfits to help you make the most of it. All the organisations mentioned below have instructors trained through PADI (Professional Association of Diving Instructors); check www.padi.com for details.

Diving Center Fornells (Passeig Marítim 68, tel: 971 376 431, www.divingfornells.com) offers diving trips in the protected Northern Reserve, as well as courses and equipment hire, and also has kayaks for hire. **S'Algar Diving** (Passeig Marítim, s/n, tel: 971 150 601, www.salgardiving.com) in the southeast takes you to some of the most beautiful diving spots on the island. **Diving Centre Poseidon** of Cala Santandria (Carrer dels Suissos 3, Ciutadella, tel: 971 382 644, www.bahia-poseidon.de) is popular, too. There are also daily snorkelling courses for children and beginners and all the necessary equipment is for hire. **Scuba Plus** (Cala'n Busquets 10, Ciutadella, tel: 696 903 160, www.scubaplus. org) runs trips for qualified divers and courses for beginners also in the north of the island and hires equipment. **Dive Inn Menorca** in Ciutadella (Passeing Es Pla de Sant Joan 10, tel: 651 644 319, www.diveinnmenorca.com) and **Bluewater Scuba** (c/Llevant Centro Civico Local 3, Cala'n Bosc, tel: 971 387 183, www.bluewaterscuba.co.uk) are another popular organisations.

BOAT TRIPS AND BOAT HIRE

The glass-bottomed **Yellow Catamarans** (tel: 639 676 351, www.yellowcatamarans.com) run one-hour trips around Maó's harbour up to eight times a day from their base in Port de Maó. From Ciutadella, the *Fiesta Rojo* (tel: 670 214 322, www.rutasmaritimasdelacruz.com) makes day trips to the southern beaches with a stop for a paella and sangria lunch and a swim. In the southwest corner, **Amigos** (tel: 618 348 006, www.holidaylinesmenorca.com) run glass-bottomed boat trips from Cala en Bosc to Cala Trebaluger and Binigaus. There are half-day trips and 'sunset parties' (weather conditions permitting), and you can snorkel from the boat if you bring your own gear. From Es Grau, in the Parc Natural de S'Albufera, trips in glass-bottomed boats can be taken out to little Illa d'en Colom and around the estuary (boatmen wait at the harbour; there is no need to book).

Sailing and motor boats can be hired from **Nautic Fun** (Moll de Levant 57, Maó, tel: 971 364 250, www.nauticfunmenorca. com). They also run sailing courses and organise fishing charters. Motor boats are also for hire from **Menorca boats** (Passeig Moll 78, Ciutadella; tel: 971 484 281, www.menorca boats.com).

KAYAKING

Kayaking is becoming increasingly popular. **Dia Complert Esport d'Aventura** (Passeig Marítim 41, Mercadal Fornells; tel: 609 670 996, www.diacomplert.com) is a competent organisation that organises kayaking trips in the north of the island.

HIKING

Whether you prefer coastal paths, undulating hills, limestone gorges or tranquil wetlands, hiking – *senderismo* in Spanish – is a delight, especially in spring and autumn. In the southeast, parts of the Camí de Cavalls, the old bridle path that used to run all round the island, can be walked, but much of it is inaccessible. Most hikes are fairly gentle and can be done by any reasonably fit person.

Dia Complert Esport d'Aventura in Fornells arranges hiking and biking routes all over the island, including birdwatching excursions. On the south coast, hiking in the Barranc d'Algendar can be organised in Cala Santa Galdana through the **Hotel Cala Galdana** (tel: 971 154 500, www.hotelcalagaldana.com). For all kinds of outdoor activities, **Menorcaactiva** (tel: 971 352 464 (Maó), or 971 381 550 (Ciutadella), www.menorcaactiva.com), is an outfit worth contacting.

Harness racing

Harness racing, or trotting, where jockeys sit in small carts from which they control their horses, is a popular spectator sport. Weekly events are organised at the Hipódromo Municipal de Maó on the road from Maó to Sant Lluís (tel: 971 365 730; www.hipodrom municipaldemao.cat), and the Hipódromo Torre del Ram in Cala en Blanes near Ciutadella (Sun afternoon; tel: 971 388 038). It's fun to watch and you can bet if you want to.

RIDING

Menorca is a great place for horses, and riding – either by the hour or on day-long treks – can be organised at a number of stables, including the **Club Hipic Ciutadella** (tel: 971 091 510, mobile: 678 859 345) at Km 4 Ctra Cala Morrell and **Rutas Ecuestres Son Olivar** (Carretera Ciutadella–Cala en Bosc Km 6, tel: 655 262 577). **Menorca a Cavall**, at Finca Santa Rita (Carretera Maó–Ciutadella Km 24, tel:

Pony trekking

971 374 637, www.menorcaacavall.com) and **Son Bou Rutas a Caballo** (c/Atalis, Torre Soli Nou, Alaior, tel: 619 841 521, www. sonbourutasacaballo.com) organise treks through woodland and along the Cami de Cavalls, the 'horse path' around the island.

CYCLING

Cyclists can take to the inland hills or deep *barrancos* (gorges) on mountain bikes, or simply enjoy coastal paths and wetland trails on conventional cycles. Many resort hotels rent bikes of various kinds. Mountain bikes can be hired in Cala Santa Galdana through the **Rtm Audax Hotel** (tel: 971 154 646, www. artiemhotels.com) who arrange a number of outdoor and sporting activities. Or you could go to **Bike Menorca** (in Maó: Avinguda Francesc Femenies 44, tel: 971 353 798, www.bike menorca.com). **Dia Complert Esport d'Aventura** in Fornells can also organise cycling routes.

Parc Natural de S'Albufera des Grau

BIRDWATCHING

Menorca is a fantastic place for birdwatching, especially in spring and autumn when numerous migrant species break their journeys here. The best sites are the protected wetlands of the **Parc Natural de S'Albufera des Grau** (tel: 971 177 705, http://balearsnatura.com), where cormorants and spoonbills are among the migrants, and booted eagles can be seen in winter, and the **Barranc d'Algendar** in the south (near Cala Santa Galdana), where kestrels and kites are commonly seen wheeling overhead.

GOLF

Menorca has one 18-hole, par 72 course, **Golf Son Parc** (tel: 971 188 875, www.golfsonparc.com), on the northeast coast, adjacent to the urbanisation of the same name. They organise golfing holidays, including 'Learn Golf in a Week' packages.

CHILDREN'S MENORCA

Menorca is a good place to take small children, as the safe, shallow waters and clean sands keep them happy for hours, and the islanders are welcoming and very child-friendly. The following is a selection of things to do when the beach begins to pall. Boat trips are always popular, and while an hour-long trip around Maó's harbour may not inspire children with an interest in naval history, there's much to see, from ruined castles to giant cruise ships, and the sea bed to examine from an observation gallery when you reach the mouth of the harbour. **Yellow Catamarans** (tel: 639 676 351) is the best known of several companies that run regular one-hour trips.

Water parks are always popular in hot weather, and **Aqua Center** in Urbanización Los Delfines (Cala en Blanes, tel: 971 388 705, May–Sept daily 10.30am–6.30pm, www.aquacenter-menorca. com) has, as it claims, something for all the family, with hydro-tubes, a giant toboggan, a children's water chute and bouncy castles, as well as a jacuzzi for parents. **Aquarock** (Cala en Bosc, tel: 971 387 822, May–Oct daily 10.30am–6pm, except Sat on May, June and Sept, www.aqua rock-menorca.com) has all the usual water park

Watery fun at Aqua Center

diversions, while **Club San Jaime** in Sant Jaume Mediterrani, near Son Bou (tel: 971 372 787, May–Oct daily 10am–7pm, www. clubsanjaime.es) has a large water chute and a wooden maze, among numerous other attractions.

At **Son Olivar Nou** there are donkeys, ponies, goats, pigs and chickens, as well as pony rides, to keep smaller children amused.

On the Carretera Ferreries–Cala Santa Galdana are two places that put on regular spectacular equestrian shows, which are suitable for children and adults during the summer months. **Son Martorellet** (tel: 971 373 406, www.sonmartorellet.com) and the **Escola Equestre Menorquina** (tel: 607 496 824) offer similar shows, although the former is larger, more elaborate and rather more expensive. It is also possible to visit the stables and watch the horses being put through their paces.

Both Aquapark and Aquarock have go-kart tracks, and **Karting Menorca** (tel: 971 380 424, daily 10am–7pm, www.castillo menorca.com), located in the big El Castillo shopping and leisure complex on the Carretera Maó–Ciutadella (Me-1), about 12km (7.5 miles) east of Ciutadella, is hard to miss.

SHOPPING

LEATHER

The best things to buy in Menorca are leather goods – the island is justly famous for its long-established leather industry. Shoes, bags and belts are the things to go for, but coats and jackets are good value, too. Ciutadella, Ferreries and Alaior are the main centres of production. Especially interesting are *abarcas*, the flat, slipper-like sandals that have been worn by peasants for centuries. They have grown less simple in recent years, and a whole range of subtle and striking colours is now available, some with delicate handpainted patterns. Shop around, because prices vary.

Calçats Truyol is a small chain that stocks some lovely designs, with branches in Maó (Carrer d'en Deià 9) and Ferreries (Carrer Pau Pons 12). In Ciutadella, **Can Magí** (Carrer de Sant Antoni Maria Claret 54, http://can-magi.com) also has a good selection.

For classy bags and belts, visit Ciutadella's **Iñaki Sampedro** (Carrer Seminari 36, www.inakisampedro.es) or Maó's **Marisa** (Carrer Hannover 7, Costa de Sa Plaça). Internationally known **Pons Quintana** (www.ponsquintana.com) sells lovely shoes in its shops in Maó (at S'Arravaleta 21), in Ciutadella (at Contramurada 95), and in Alaior at Sant Antoni 120. **Jaime Mascaro** (www.mascaro.com) is the other well-known shoe

Crafting abarcas

company on the island, and has a shop in Maó at Carrer Ses Moreres 29. The goods you find in the Mascaro factory outlet on the Poligono Industrial, on the Me-1 near Ferreries, are not always as good as those you will find in smaller shops. This is true of all the other large-scale emporiums strung along the Me-1. Some provide restaurants and children's playgrounds to attract customers, but they are not the best places to shop.

You will see the sign **Pou Nou** (www.pounou.com) in shops all over the island. This is a Menorcan designer T-shirt company, but they also make other casual wear, and their quality, colours and designs are good. **S'Ecològica de Menorca** (www. ecologicademenorca.com) use only chlorine-free, water-based paints on their attractive T-shirts and casuals, with designs by Menorcan artist Jaume Bagur. You will find them in numerous outlets all over the island.

Traditional abarcas

FOOD AND DRINK

The food most worth taking home is cheese, **Queso de Mahón** (see page 103). It is actually made in Alaior, and you can buy it at the factory outlets there: **La Payesa**, Carrer des Banyer 64 (www.lapayesa.es) and **Coingo**, Carrer Es Mercadel 8. If you don't get to Alaior, don't worry – it is sold all over the island, and even at the airport, packed in distinctive boxes. At **Hort de Sant Patrici** (Camí de Sant Patrici, Ferreries; tel: 971 373 702, www.sant patrici.com), you can watch the cheese being made and taste it before buying.

Ensaimadas, the sugar-dusted pastries that are an island speciality, can be bought in *confiterias* (pastry shops) and speciality stores everywhere, and come in all sizes – the larger ones are often packed in special boxes. There's a good selection in the old-fashioned **Herbera**

Ensaimadas, a treat for breakfast

Bakery (Carrer de Maó 28, Ciutadella), **Panadería y Bollería Díaz** (Calle Comerciants i Botiguers 25, Ciutadella) and in **El Turronero** (Carrer Nou 22, Maó), a shop established in 1894 that also sells Xoriguer gin, Queso de Mahón, local figs and *turrón*, an almond-based delicacy, that can be soft like fudge, or hard, rather like nougat.

Cas Ferret (Carrer Josep Maria Quadrado 14) in Ciutadella has a good selection of cured Mahón cheese, cold meats and other regional products. Also in Ciutadella, **Ca Na Fayas** (Avinguida Jaume I El Conqueridor 47, www.canafayas.es) sells a range of local products, including cheese, sausages, honey and wine.

Xoriguer gin, packaged in bottles with handles on the neck, can be sampled and purchased at the Xoriguer distillery outlet, Andén Poniente 91, Maó (www.xoriguer.es), but it's available everywhere, as is *pomada*, a gin-and-lemonade drink, and a variety of colourful herbal liqueurs. Menorca is not known

Gin distillery

for its wines, but **Bodegas Binifadet** is producing some excellent vintages. Their chardonnay has received particular praise. Buy in specialist food shops or visit the winery outside San Lluis (tel: 971 150 715, www.binifadet.com) for tours and tastings.

CERAMICS

Some of the best places on the island to see and buy **pottery** and other local crafts are **Centre Artesanal de Menorca** (Carrer Metge Camps, Es Mercadal, www.artesania demenorca.com) and **Castillo Menorca** (Carretera General Maó-Ciutadella; www.castillomenorca.com). Both have interesting and unusual handmade items, although there are quite a lot of run-of-the-mill souvenirs on sale in both places as well. For more artsy products see Vico's 'creative ceramics' (www.ceramicavico.es) with stores in Maó, Fornells and Ciutadella.

MARKETS

Morning markets are held in all towns on Menorca, both outdoors or in covered market halls. They usually sell clothes, household items and sometimes craftwork as well as food. The biggest and most colourful food markets are held from Monday to Saturday in the **Claustre del Carme** in Maó and the **Plaça de la Libertat** in Ciutadella. Ferreries holds a renowned farmers' market on Friday and Saturday morning, when local produce and craftwork are for sale. Alaior's market is on Thursday, Es Castell's on Monday and Wednesday, Es Migjorn Gran's on Wednesday, Es Mercadel's on Sunday and Fornells' on Wednesday.

NIGHTLIFE AND ENTERTAINMENT

Menorca is not really the place to go for nightlife. There are clubs and discos in the bigger resorts but the island does not really attract the clubbing crowd. **Cova d'en Xoroi** disco (tel: 971 377 236, www.covadenxoroi.com), is the most unusual, dramatically set in the cliff in Cala N'Porter.

A few places worth trying in Maó are the music bar **Mambo** (Carreró d'es Muret 22), a popular Latin-American disco with hot rhythms, and **Akelaare** (Moll de Ponent 41), a vaulted cocktail bar that plays jazz, blues and modern music. In Ciutadella, try **Sa Clau Jazz Club** (www.saclau.com) in the Marina for jazz, cocktails and single-malt whiskies. **Jazzbah** (Pla de Sant Joan 4, http://www.jazzbah.es), by the port, holds popular live sessions, starting at 8pm. Also in the port is **Asere**, a lively salsa club with music every evening during the summer months. **Casino Sant Climent** (Carrer Sant Jaume 4, www.casinosant climent.com) in Sant Climent is something of an institution, and hosts good live jazz.

The only casino is **Casino Marítim** (Moll de Levant 287, Maó; tel: 971 364 962, www.casinomaritim.es; restaurant daily 6pm–2am, casino 4pm–5am). You should dress smartly and take your passport or driving licence for identification purposes.

Theatrical performances are in Spanish or Catalan, of course, but the **Teatre Principal** (tel: 971 355 603, www.teatre mao.com) stages interesting musical events, where language is not a problem.

Horsemanship at
Maó's Festa de Gràcia

FESTIVALS

Many of the festivals in Menorca revolve around the *jaleo*, a dance performed by horses, orchestrated by skilled riders – *caixers*. The two major events are the Festes de Sant Joan, in Ciutadella, and the Festes de la Vierge de Gràcia, in Maó. Sant Joan is celebrated on 23–24 June, and on the previous Sunday, the 'Día des Be', a man representing John the Baptist, dressed in sheepskins, walks barefoot through the old town of Ciutadella, inviting everyone to the fiesta. On the 23rd the celebrations start with the *primer toc*, the first notes of a flute called a *flabiol*. Then Ciutadella goes wild, with crowds of people thronging into the Plaça d'es Born and neighbouring streets to witness horseback processions and jousting tournaments. The horsemen, dressed in black and white and decorated with ribbons, embroidery and carnations, ride among the crowds, prancing and circling on their horses' hind legs. The longer a horse manages to stay on two legs, the greater the appreciation of the crowd, which surges forward, oblivious to the flailing hooves.

The festival honouring the Vierge de Gràcia in Maó on 7–9 September is equally raucous, with colourful processions and music, and similar stunning displays of horsemanship and daring in the flag-bedecked streets. Both events are crowned by magnificent firework displays on the final evening.

CALENDAR OF EVENTS

17 January: Fests d'es Tres Tocs – Festival of the Three Blows – is held in Ciutadella to commemorate the reconquest of Menorca in 1287.

Mid- to late February: Carnival (Carnaval) is celebrated in many towns and villages, with fancy dress parades and general revelry.

Late March–April: Semana Santa (Holy Week) is celebrated throughout the island with solemn processions. Festivities in Maó and Ciutadella are the most impressive.

23–24 June: Festes de Sant Joan in Ciutadella. Two days of spectacular equestrian displays, music and general fun, crowned by a magnificent fireworks display.

15–16 July: Día del Virgen de Carmen. The patron saint of fishermen and sailors is celebrated in many ports with processions of decorated boats on the water. Maó, Ciutadella and Fornells are the principal venues.

Third weekend of July: Sant Martí is celebrated in Es Mercadal with secular and religious events.

Fourth weekend of July: Festa de Sant Antoní in Fornells, in honour of the patron saint of the village. The processions are crowned by a magnificent *jaleo* (horses' dance) at the harbour.

July–September: Classical-music festivals are held on various dates throughout these summer months in Maó, Fornells and Ciutadella.

Fifth weekend of July or First weekend of August: Es Migjorn Gran celebrates its patron saint, Sant Cristòfal.

First weekend after 10 August: Sant Llorenç is celebrated in Alaior, with a pilgrimage made to Binixems.

23–25 August: Sant Bartomeu in Ferreries, with a *jaleo*.

7–9 September: Festes de la Vierge de Gràcia. The Virgin of Monte Toro is honoured with a huge celebration in Maó.

12–14 September: Sant Nicolau is celebrated in Es Mercadal and El Toro with processions, a *jaleo*, music and folk dancing, as well as a religious ceremony at the sanctuary on top of Monte El Toro.

Late September: The British Fair in Maó showing the British influence on the town. Parades, tours and historical re-enactments.

EATING OUT

Those who find food one of the greatest pleasures of foreign travel will not be disappointed in Menorca. Whether you are eating out in restaurants or buying food in local markets to cook in the kitchen of your self-catering apartment, or take on picnics, you'll find the choice wide and interesting. You won't find the best of it in the resort restaurants catering mainly to northern European tourists, which tend to fall back on 'international cuisine', but steer clear of these and you will find plenty of places serving good, authentic food. You may also find, when wandering past a row of harbourside restaurants, that their menus look pretty much the same, and there is little – including the price – to tell you which is superior to its neighbour. The clientele is a fairly reliable guide: too few customers is a bad sign, of course, but a very full restaurant may be one that caters largely to tour groups, and the food may therefore be rather bland. The number of Spanish- or Catalan-speakers eating in an establishment usually indicates that the food and service are good and that you will get value for money.

Richelieu's sauce

Salsa mahonesa – mayonnaise – originated on the island in the 18th century. The story goes that a local chef made it for the Duke of Richelieu, leader of the French forces that drove the British from the island in 1756, and he took the recipe back to Paris with him. In another version, the cook was Richelieu's mistress, and he named it after her – *la mahonesa*.

CUINA MENORQUINA

It is in restaurants advertising *cuina menorquina* that you will find the true island food. *Tumbet* is a dish of

A beautiful setting for lunch

peppers, aubergines, tomatoes and potatoes, coated in beaten egg and baked in the oven. This often features as a first course, but can be very filling, so should be followed by something light. *Trempó* is also served as a first course: described as a salad, it can be more like a rather solid *gazpacho*, made of finely chopped tomatoes, peppers, onions, capers and lots of garlic in oil and vinegar – good, as long as you really like garlic. Don't get confused with *coca de trempó*, which is a kind of pizza with tomatoes, green peppers and onions. *Conejo con higos* (rabbit with dried figs), *cordero con cebollas y alcaparras* (lamb with onions and capers) and *cabrito al horno* (roast kid) are substantial and delicious oven-baked dishes. *Escaldums*, a stew of chicken, meat balls, potatoes and vegetables, is tasty and very filling. *Berenjenos relleños* (stuffed aubergines) are also very popular. Queso de Mahón (see page 103) is often used in salads or melted on baked vegetables. *Espinacas à la catalana* – spinach cooked with garlic, anchovies, raisins and pine nuts – is a first course found on many menus.

Soups are popular, too, including *escudella*, a soup of mixed vegetables, and *sopas mallorquinas* (a Mallorcan dish always referred to in this plural form). The latter is a combination of vegetables, olives, garlic and sometimes pork, more like a stew than a soup, and a substantial first course.

FISH DISHES

In most island restaurants, but especially those in Maó, Ciutadella and Fornells, you will find a wide range of fresh fish *(pescado)* on offer, in many guises. *Lubina* (sea bass), *dorado* (gilthead bream) and *besugo* (sea bream) are cooked either on a grill *(a la plancha)* or in the oven *(al horno)*. They are often

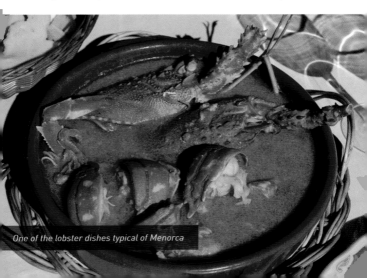

One of the lobster dishes typical of Menorca

prepared in an outer casing of sea salt before being baked; you would imagine this would make the fish very salty but it doesn't, and the taste is delicious. *Sardinas a la plancha* (grilled sardines) are found on many menus. A *parillada de pescado* is a mixture of grilled fish. *Suquet* is a rich fish stew, and *bacalao* is cod, salted and dried. It is not to everyone's taste, but when well prepared it can be good, especially in *esqueixada*, a salad of tomatoes, onions and shredded salt cod.

Calamares (squid), *sepia* (cuttlefish) and *pulpo* (octopus), cooked in a variety of ways, are widely available. *Calamares en su tinta* is squid cooked in its own ink; *a la romana* means it is cut into rings and fried in batter.

Caldereta de llagosta is the star among Menorcan fish dishes. It is the speciality of the fish restaurants of Fornells, but also features on menus in the port of Maó and Ciutadella. A thick stew is prepared using lobster, tomatoes, onions, green pepper, garlic, parsley, egg yolk and brandy, then poured on to slices of bread and served. Cooks all have their own recipes, so the dish is never quite the same from place to place. It is rich and delicious and the only disadvantage is the price – around €50–55 a person, and it is always made for two.

There are two cheaper variations, however: *caldereta de mariscos*, a thick shellfish soup, and *caldereta de pescado*, which contains several different kinds of fish.

PUDDINGS AND PASTRIES

Home-made *crème caramel*, *crema Catalana*, or its mass-produced cousin, known as a *flan*, is as ubiquitous on the Balearics as the mainland, but there are also some wonderful sweet pastries and the almond-and-honey desserts that are a delicious legacy of the Moorish occupation. *Ensaimadas* are the pastries you are most likely to see on sale, a light and airy concoction

The island's famous cheese

that's rolled up like a turban, dusted with sugar, and often eaten for breakfast. Large, family-sized versions are also sold, sometimes in plywood boxes, and these make attractive, typically Menorcan gifts to take home if you have room in your luggage. Vegetarians should be aware that lard *(saim)* is an essential Menorcan ingredient and a key element in the *ensaimada*. *Crespells*, a kind of shortbread biscuit, and *amargos* almond-flavoured biscuits are also popular.

SHOPPING FOR FOOD

If you are on a self-catering holiday and shopping for food in the markets, you will be able to choose from a wide variety of vegetables, depending on the season. Glossy aubergines, large, misshapen but delicious tomatoes and courgettes, and wonderfully fresh spinach will help you make authentic Mediterranean dishes to accompany the fresh fish that glistens on beds of ice, or meat, which is cut to order by the butcher. If you are making up a picnic, local cheese, chorizo, tomatoes and seasonal fruit, together with a loaf of fresh bread, may be all you need.

EATING HABITS

As in the rest of Spain, people in Menorca tend to eat late: lunch is generally between 1.30 and 3.30pm, and 10pm is a popular time for dinner. However, restaurateurs, well aware that Northern European visitors prefer to eat earlier, have adapted their timetables accordingly, and some serve food throughout the day. Remember not to write off a restaurant that looks alarmingly empty at 8.30pm because it may be buzzing with local people and visitors two hours later. Be aware that many restaurants close for several months in winter and many close one day a week, usually Monday or Tuesday.

Many places offer a *menú del día*, a daily set menu that is a real bargain; it is always available at lunchtime and sometimes in the evening too. For a fixed price (around €15), you will get three courses – a starter, which is often soup or salad, a main fish or meat dish and a dessert, generally ice cream, a piece of

⊘ QUESO DE MAHÓN

The British introduced the dairy industry to Menorca in the 18th century, and it flourished. Not only will you see lots of cows as you travel around the island, but also many huge advertisements for cheese – Queso de Mahón. Despite the name, most of it is made in Alaior and despite mechanisation, most is still made in the traditional manner. It is produced from cow's milk with just a little ewe's milk added, which gives it a distinctive flavour. The whey is separated from the set milk and the cheese is soaked for a day in salt water and left for a month on a rack, where it is turned regularly. The varieties depend on how long they have aged, so you get *tierno* (young), *semi-curado* (semi-mature), *curado* (mature) and *añejo* (very mature indeed), with a texture similar to parmesan. You can buy it in any grocer's or gift shop, or even at the airport, but for details of the factory outlets in Alaior, see page 51.

fruit or a *flan* (caramel custard), plus a glass of wine, beer or bottled water and bread.

Reservations are recommended only at more expensive restaurants, or at Sunday lunchtime in popular spots. Prices sometimes include service – look for *servicio incluido* on the bill – but if not it is customary to leave a 10 percent tip.

TAPAS

Tapas, the popular Spanish snacks, have not caught on in Menorca as they have in other parts of Spain. You do find some tapas bars, though – more in Ciutadella than in Maó. *Calamares* (squid), *albóndigas* (meat balls), spicy *chorizo* and *boquerones* (marinated anchovy fillets), are among the most ubiquitous, often accompanied by *pa amb tomàquet*, bread rubbed with oil, garlic and tomato.

DRINKS

Wine is usually drunk with meals, much of it imported from the Spanish mainland; riojas and varieties from the Catalan Penedès region feature prominently. There is virtually no wine made commercially on Menorca; you will sometimes, but not often, see Mallorcan wines, most of which come from the region around Binissalem. Spanish beer is also popular, especially with young people. Fresh orange juice *(zumo de naranja)* is refreshing, and those who like the flavour of almonds should try *horchata de chufa*, a milky drink made from ground almonds that is served ice cold in summer.

Locally made Xoriguer gin is sold everywhere, but waiters will often ask visitors if they would prefer one of the more expensive internationally known brands. Ask for *nacional* if you want to try the island gin. You will also see *pomada*, which is gin mixed with lemonade. There are lots of herbal liqueurs – *hierbas* – as well, which sometimes come in frighteningly vivid colours.

Xoriguer gin and pomada for sale

GIN 10€

POMADA

Coffee is drunk at breakfast and throughout the day. *Café con leche* is a large one with lots of hot milk; with a *cortado*, usually served in a glass, you get the same amount of coffee with just a splash of milk. A *café solo* is a small, strong black coffee, and with an *americano* you get added hot water.

BARS AND CAFÉS

In towns, some bars and cafés open at first light to cater for early-morning workers, and the majority are open by 8.30am for breakfast. One of the great pleasures of the Mediterranean is sitting in a square in the morning with a coffee and croissant and watching a town come to life. In resorts, however, where most tourists breakfast in their hotels, you may have more difficulty finding somewhere for an early coffee. At many open-air cafés you can get a selection of sandwiches – *bocadillos* in Spanish, *entrepans* in Catalan – at most hours.

TO HELP YOU ORDER

Could we have a table, please? **¿Nos puede dar una mesa, por favor?**

Do you have a set menu? **¿Tiene un menú del día?**

I'd like... **Quiero...**

The bill, please **La cuenta, por favor**

MENU READER

agua water
vino wine
leche milk
cerveza beer
pan bread
ensalada salad
tortilla omelette
pescado fish
mariscos shellfish
langosta lobster
calamares squid
mejillones mussels
anchoas anchovies
atún tuna
bacalao dried cod
cangrejo crab
pulpo octopus
trucha trout
carne meat
cerdo/lomo pork
ternera veal
cordero lamb
buey/res beef
pollo chicken

conejo rabbit
poco hecho rare
al punto medium
bien hecho well done
asado roast
a la plancha grilled
al ajillo in garlic
picante spicy
salsa sauce
cocido stew
jamón serrano cured ham
chorizo spicy sausage
bocadillo sandwich
arroz rice
verduras vegetables
champiñones mushrooms
habas broad beans
espinacas spinach
cebollas onions
queso cheese
postre dessert
helado ice cream
azúcar sugar
flan caramel custard

PLACES TO EAT

We have used the following symbols to give an idea of the price for a three-course meal for one, including wine, cover and service:

€€€   45–75 euros
€€   30–45 euros
€   below 30 euros

MAÓ AND ES CASTELL

Can Vermut €€ *Moll de Llevant 176, tel: 971 361 726,* www.canvermut. com. Nice atmosphere, good prices and delicious dishes, such as *lasaña de berenjenas* (aubergine lasagna) and other tapas, make it a very popular spot to hang out with friends. Open Wed–Sun noon–4pm and 9pm–1am, with live music on Sundays.

El Cachito €€ *Moll de Llevant 278, tel: 971 369 792,* www.elcachito menorca.com. This pleasant and colourful restaurant serves up its own versions of traditional dishes. *Calamares a la plancha* (grilled squid) and *rodaballo frito* (fried turbot) are all-time favourites.

Il Porto 225 €€ *Moll de Llevant 225, tel: 971 483 428,* http://ilporto225. com. Come here for a relaxed atmosphere, good Italian food and an excellent wine list. The fish dishes are particularly good.

La Josefina €€ *Carrer Ruiz i Pablo 95, Es Castell, tel: 971 354 950.* The menu of this restaurant set above the harbour Cales Fonts, reflects the daily catch of local fishermen. The pleasant, open-air interior patio is a great place for summer evening meals. Open daily in summer, in winter closed Sun and Mon dinner.

La Minerva €€€ *Moll de Llevant 87, tel: 971 351 995,* http://restaurantela minerva.es. The main restaurant is set in an old flour mill, but you can also eat on the floating jetty. Elegant and expensive, although the tasting menu offers excellent value.

La Mojigata Café €€ *Plaça d'Espanya 15, tel: 971 360 870*. This informal restaurant opened by Daniel Gonzalez Mora, chef at the famous Sa Pedrera des Pujol (see page 112), serves good food all day from early breakfast until late supper. Great views from the terrace over the fish market and wide selection of tapas and wine.

Nou Siroco €–€€ *Moll des Cales Fonts 39, Cales Fonts, Es Castell, tel: 971 367 965*. Reasonable food at reasonable prices, served by friendly staff – a formula that seems to work, judging by the number of regular customers. Paella is popular, and you could make a whole meal of the tapas-style starters.

Roma € *Moll de Llevant 295, tel: 971 353 777*, www.restaurantepizzeriaroma. com. Excellent pizzas, pasta and other Italian specialities, fair prices and a cheerful atmosphere ensure that it's always busy. Serves also vegetarian and gluten-free dishes. Open Wed–Mon from 12.30pm to midnight.

Ses Forquilles €€ *Rovellada de Dalt 20, tel: 971 356 983*, www.sesforquilles. com. Offers great modern food based on traditional recipes and local ingredients of excellent quality. It has two separate spaces, the one downstairs is more informal. Open daily except Sun and Mon in winter.

S'Espigó €€€ *Moll de Llevant 267, tel: 971 369 909*, www.sespigo.com. Another reliably good harbourside restaurant, specialising mostly in fish and seafood. Try the artichokes with prawns or baby peppers stuffed with fish for starters. Closed Sun and Mon lunch.

Treból €€ *Moll des Cales Fonts 43, Cales Fonts, Es Castell, tel: 971 367 097*, www.trebolmenorca.es. A long-established and popular fish restaurant built into the cliff on the attractive Cales Fonts harbour side. It's a good place to taste *caldereta de langosta*. Open daily in summer 1–3.30pm and 7.30pm–1am.

Varadero €€€ *Moll de Llevant 4, tel: 971 352 074*. Beside the Port Authority building this minimalist restaurant has a menu that includes salmon cooked in cava. To enjoy the view and spend less, check *Menu Tapas* or *Menu del día*.

CIUTADELLA

Café Balear €€ *Pla de Sant Joan 15, Port de Ciutadella, tel: 971 380 005,* www.cafe-balear.com. An excellent little restaurant at the east end of the harbour, just past the pedestrian bridge. Some say that the *caldereta de llagosta* (lobster stew) is the best in Menorca. There's a delicious choice of starters, from *gambas a la plancha* (grilled prawns) to *calamares rebozados* (squid in batter).

Ca'n Nito € *Plaça des Born 11, tel: 971 480 768.* An unassuming café on the square that serves good tapas day and night. The anchovies *(anchoas)* are recommended.

Casa Manolo €€–€€€ *Carrer Marina 117, Port de Ciutadella, tel: 971 380 003.* At the far end of the harbour promenade, Manolo's has been established for nearly as long as the port – well, for over four decades anyway. There's a wide choice of freshly caught fish, from clams to *caldereta de llagosta.*

D'es Port €€ *Carrer Marina 23, Port de Ciutadella, tel: 971 480 022.* Set into the cliff and with tables on the quayside, this smart blue-and-white restaurant serves excellent fish. As well as *caldereta de llagosta* there's *suquet* (fish stew), *paella*, of course, and *esqueixada*, a salad of tomatoes, onions and salt cod. Service is attentive.

El Horno €€ *Carrer des Forn 12, tel: 971 380 767,* www.elhorno.biz. If you can tear yourself away from sunset over the harbour – which can be difficult on a lovely evening – this small basement restaurant tucked into a narrow street at the back of Plaça d'es Born serves fresh fish every day as well as French dishes.

Fang i Aram € *Carrer Martí I Bella 11, tel 971 34 871,* www.restaurante vegetarianomenorca.com. The first vegetarian restaurant in Menorca offers everything you would expect: hummus, guacamole, salads, rice and wok dishes. A good set menu costs only €14.

La Guitarra €€ *Carrer dels Dolors 1, tel: 971 381 355.* Another place that makes it worth leaving the harbour. Close to the Plaça de la Catedral, this well-run and long-established cellar restaurant serves authentic *cuina menorquina: conejo con cebollas* (rabbit with onions), *escaldums* (chicken, meatballs and vegetables) and much more. Closed on Sun.

Mon €€€ *Paseo Sant Nicolau 4, tel: 971 381 718,* www.canfaustino.com. Felipe Llufriu, the Michelin-star chef of this elegant restaurant set in a beautiful house with a small terrace, specialises in local and seasonal products. Booking is advisable. Closed Sun.

Smoix €€ *Av. Jaume Conqueridor 38, tel: 971 382 808,* www.smoix.com. Located in the centre of Ciutadella this modern restaurant offers mostly Mediterranean cooking with a contemporary twist. The set menu starts from €16.50. Closed on Mondays.

THE NORTHEAST
Es Grau

Tamarindos €–€€ *Pas d'es Tamarells 14, tel: 971 359 420,* www.barrest aurantetamarindos.es. The fish dishes in this unpretentious little place are wholesome, simple and taste all the better for being served on a wooden terrace so close to the sea you could almost catch them yourself.

FORNELLS

Ca Na Marga €€ *Urbanización Ses Salines 1, tel: 971 376 410,* www.cana marga.com. This big airy restaurant is an excellent place to eat grilled meat, but the pizzas and other Mediterranean dishes are also very tasty. From May to October open every evening from 7.30pm.

Es Cranc €€€ *Carrer Escoles 31, tel: 971 376 442.* Tucked away in the old town, but only a few minutes' walk from the harbour, Es Cranc serves imaginative meat dishes, fresh fish and seafood. Popular with islanders and visitors from Barcelona, so it's best to book at weekends. Open daily lunch and dinner.

Es Cranc Pelut €€€ *Gumersindo Riera 98 (Passeig Marítim), tel: 971 376 743*. Despite the confusingly similar name (Es Cranc means 'The Crab' and this is 'The Hairy Crab'), the two restaurants are quite different. On the seafront, this one specialises in *caldereta de llagosta* and other seafood, and its renowned chef, Diego Coll, has produced a book on Menorcan cooking. Open May–Oct.

Es Port €€ *Carrer Gumersindo Riera 5 (Passeig Marítim), tel: 971 376 403*. Friendly and extremely relaxed, this harbourside restaurant makes a delicious *caldereta*. The *lubina* (sea bass) and *dorada* (gilthead bream), baked in a crust of salt, are excellent, too, and come at considerably more affordable prices.

Sa Llagosta €€€ *Carrer Gabriel Gelabert 12, tel: 971 376 566*. Very smart and discreet, this establishment serves *calamares* with green risotto, and baked fish dishes, including *rodaballo* (turbot) and *pargo* (sea bream), as well as lobster in many guises, including *caldereta de llagosta* (lobster stew). Open daily for lunch and dinner.

Sa Mesquida

Cap Roig €€€ *Carretera Sa Mesquida 13, tel: 971 188 383*, www.restaurant caproig.com. Set above the harbour cliff not far from Maó, this smart restaurant specialises in fish and seafood. Prices are not low, but the setting and an excellent view of Cala Mesquida make it worth a visit, especially at sunset. Booking is recommended. Open daily noon–midnight Easter–15 Oct.

THE SOUTH
Cala Blanca

Es Caliu €€ *Carretera Ciutadella–Cala en Bosc, tel: 971 380 165*, www.restaurantegrillescaliu.com. Good barbecued meat is the speciality of this big, busy restaurant. Apr–Oct open daily, Nov–Mar only Fri–Sun.

Cala en Bosc

La Marina €€ *Paeo Portixol local 18, Cala'n Bosch, tel: 971 387 411.* Located in the marina (as the name suggests), this welcoming restaurant is known for its excellent fish and seafood fare. The menu includes lemon sole, garlic prawns, spider crab stew, paella and more – prepared in a variety of imaginative ways. For something more fortifying, try the excellent lamb. Good local wines. Open daily from noon until 11pm. Extensive children's menu.

Sant Lluís

Pan y Vino €€ *Camí de la Coixa 3, Torret, tel: 971 150 201,* www.panyvino menorca.com. Located in the village of Torret, just to the south of Sant Lluís, this intimate restaurant has a French chef, and serves excellent oven-baked fish and meat and game dishes. It is very popular with the local expatriates, so booking is advisable. Open summer for dinner Wed–Mon, spring also for Sunday lunch. Closed Dec–Jan.

Sa Pedrera d'es Pujol €€€ *Cami des Pujol 14 Torret, tel: 971 150 717,* www.sapedreradespujol.com. Set in an old quarry, this is arguably the best restaurant in Menorca thanks to the creative cuisine of Daniel González Mora. The great tasting menu based on regional products costs around €70 (the shorter version only €40). The long list of wines (300 no less) is extraordinary.

THE CENTRE

Es Mercadal

Ca n'Aguedet €€ *Carrer Lepanto 30, tel: 971 375 391.* Some of the island's best *cuina menorquina* in a restaurant that has been here since 1936. Rabbit, lamb and suckling pig *(lechona)* among other things are served in a light and airy first-floor dining room. Surprisingly reasonable prices. Booking advisable.

Ca n'Olga €€ *Pont Na Macarrana, tel: 971 375 459.* Set near the river, this place serves good *cuina menorquina* on a large terrace or in a stylish dining room. *Mariscos* (seafood), *cordoniz* (quail) and *conejo* (rabbit) are all recommended, and *Cap Roig* (scorpion fish) is one of the house specialities. Booking is advisable.

Molí d'es Racó €€ *Carrer Major 53, tel: 971 375 275*. Set in an old mill with a large terrace, just off the Me-1. The Menorcan cooking is good, but note that the restaurant caters to large coach parties. Daily for lunch and dinner.

Tast €€€ *Plaça Pere Camps 21, tel: 971 375 587, www.tastmercadal.com*. A good place to taste traditional Menorcan cuisine with a modern twist. The set menus are the best options, otherwise choose from a great selection of creative tapas at an affordable price.

Es Migjorn Gran

S'Engolidor €€ *Carrer Major 3, tel: 971 370 193, www.sengolidor.es*. Islanders and visitors come from far and wide to eat here. In a series of little dining rooms and alcoves or outside on a shady terrace, attentive and friendly waiters serve delicious *cuina menorquina*, including *dorado con alcaparras* (gilthead bream with capers) and *conejo con mostaza* (rabbit with mustard sauce) as well as home-made desserts. From the terrace there are wonderful views over the S'Engolidor *barranco*. Booking is essential. Apr–Oct Tue–Sun; serves dinner only plus Sunday lunch.

FERRERIES

Mesón El Gallo €€ *Carretera Cala Galdana Km 1.5, tel: 971 373 039, www.mesonelgallo.com*. This farmhouse restaurant just outside town on the way to Cala Galdana has been in business for many years. It is renowned for its good-quality grilled meat, but the paella is also one of the specialities of the house. Apr–Oct Tue–Sun for lunch and dinner.

A–Z TRAVEL TIPS

A SUMMARY OF PRACTICAL INFORMATION

A

ACCOMMODATION (See Recommended Hotels on page 134)

Hotel prices are not government controlled, but rates have to be posted at reception desks and in rooms. Off-season, you can get much lower rates but many hotels close from November to Easter. In high season, many resort hotels are block-booked by tour operators.

Accommodation ranges across a broad spectrum, although there are not that many *pensions* (guest houses). *Hostales* (modest hotels) are graded from one to three stars while *hoteles* (hotels) are rated from one to five stars. Grades are more a reflection of facilities than quality: some two-star places can be superior to others with four. There is a blurring of categories, however: *pensions* may call themselves *hostales* and vice-versa; some hotels also call themselves *hostales*.

Small hotels in rural settings and refurbished farmhouses and manor houses are called *finca* or *agroturisme* properties. They range from rustic to luxurious; many have pools and tennis courts. Some are listed at www.menorcaturismorural.net.

Package deals are the cheapest way to holiday in Menorca; accommodation is nearly always in the busiest resorts, but can provide an economical base from which to explore the island. Packages offering accommodation in furnished apartments or villas are also popular. They are usually part of a complex with amenities, such as a pool, gardens and sports facilities.

I would like a single/double room **Quisiera una habitación sencilla/doble**
with/without bathroom and toilet/shower **con/sin baño/ducha**
What's the rate per night? **¿Cuál es el precio por noche?**
Is breakfast included? **¿Está incluído el desayuno?**

AIRPORT

Maó's compact little airport (MAH) is 5km (3 miles) from the city centre. It is about a 15-minute taxi ride (around €10; Maó tel: 971 367 111 and Ciutadella tel: 971 382 896). The airport bus service to Maó (€2.65 one way) runs every 30 minutes in summer and every hour in winter. For more information and airport maps go to www.aena.es/es/aeropuerto-menorca/index.html.

B

BICYCLE AND SCOOTER HIRE

Bikes can be hired in most of the resorts – hotels and tourist offices have leaflets, and you'll be handed flyers in the street. In Maó, contact Bike Menorca (Av. Francesc Femenies 44, tel: 971 353 798, www.bike menorca.com). Mopeds and scooters are also available in most resorts, but you need a licence. A helmet is compulsory when riding a motorcycle. Ask the bike shop for a helmet and for a pump and puncture kit, in case you get stuck with a flat tyre.

BUDGETING FOR YOUR TRIP

All prices below are approximate and given only as a guide.

Accommodation. Rates for a double room in high season can range from as low as €50 per night in a *hostal* to as much as over €200 at a top-of-the-range hotel. A comfortable 3-star hotel costs approximately €80–125. Rates drop considerably out of season.

Attractions. Most museums and megalithic sites charge an entry fee of around €3–8. Water parks are around €10 for under-11s, €20 for over-11s, but a family could easily spend a whole day in them.

Getting there. Air fares vary enormously. Flights from the UK with a budget airline can vary from around £75 return off-season to £150 or more in high season. From the US, flights cost approximately $1,000 return to Palma or Madrid, from where you get a connecting flight.

Ferries. Inter-island ferries between Menorca (Ciutadella) and Mallorca (Port d'Alcúdia) cost about €40 return for foot passengers, and from about €150 to €300 for a car and two passengers. Ferries from Palma (Mallorca) to Maó (Menorca) cost about €60 return for foot passengers. For details, see ferry companies websites: Balearia (www.balearia. com) and Trasmediterranea (www.trasmediterranea.es).

Meals. *A menú del día*, a fixed-price meal, is an excellent bargain, usually costing no more than €15 for a reasonably good three-course meal with one drink included. The average price of a three-course meal, à la carte, including house wine, will be about €30–45 per person. You can pay considerably less, but at the top restaurants you will pay a lot more (see page 107).

C

CAMPING

Pitching a tent on beaches and parkland is illegal and a number of people are prosecuted every year for illegal camping. You may be able to camp on private land if you ask permission first.

Menorca has two official camp sites. The first is S'Atalaia (Carretera Ferreries–Cala Galdana, tel: 971 374 232; www.campingsatalaia. com; Apr–Sept), set in pine woods 4km (2.5 miles) from Ferreries and 3km (2 miles) from the beach at Cala Galdana. Son Bou (Carretera Sant Jaume–Alaior, tel: 971 372 605/971 372 727; www.campingsonbou.com; end of Apr–Oct), is 2.5km (1.5 miles) from the beach. Facilities at both sites include a pool, showers, restaurant/bar and supermarket; advance booking is advisable.

CAR HIRE

The bus service is good, but if you want to travel around a good deal, renting a car is advisable. Major international companies – Avis, Hertz, Europcar – and Spanish national companies have offices at the airport and in Maó as well as in the major resorts. Rates are seasonal, and much lower out of season, and at any time if organised in advance, especially over the internet. You may pay around €60 a day for an economy model in high season, but you get a much better deal if you book for a week. Third-party insurance is included by law, but comprehensive insurance – *todo riesgo* – may be extra. Insurance may not cover you for off-road driving, even in a four-wheel-drive vehicle. Most types of car are available, but the vast majority are small, economy models. Hirers must be at least 21 and have held a licence for a year. You need only your national driving licence if you are travelling from another EU country (some companies require international licences from those who are not).

> I'd like to rent a car for one day/week. **Quisiera alquilar un coche por un día/una semana.**
> Please include full insurance. **Haga el favor de incluir el seguro a todo riesgo.**

CLIMATE

The sea is pleasantly warm for swimming from June to October. Temperatures in July and August can be scorching, and humidity may be high. Menorca enjoys a mild winter, although it can be swept by cold winds, especially in the north, where the Tramuntana can be fierce. Although many hotels still close in winter, the tourist season is getting longer: spring and autumn are mild and pleasant and popular with walkers and birdwatchers.

The chart below shows the average monthly temperatures; these do not vary greatly, except in the mountainous areas.

	J	F	M	A	M	J	J	A	S	O	N	D
°C	10	11	12	14	17	22	24	24	22	18	14	12
°F	50	51	54	58	63	71	76	76	72	65	57	53

CLOTHING

In summer you only need lightweight cotton clothes, although in June and September a jacket or sweater is useful for the evening. Take a sunhat and something with sleeves to cover your shoulders against the midday sun. During the rest of the year a jacket and umbrella will come in handy. Although the prevailing attitude is towards casual dress, some restaurants, bars and clubs object to men wearing shorts and T-shirts, and women being too skimpily dressed. Don't offend local sensibilities by wearing swimwear or very skimpy clothing in city streets, museums or churches. Walking shoes or trainers are advisable, of course, if you are planning long treks, as is a small backpack to carry lightweight anoraks and refreshments.

CRIME AND SAFETY

Spain's crime rate has caught up with that of other European countries, and the Balearics have not been immune, although they remain one of the safest places in Europe. Be on your guard against purse-snatchers and pickpockets around major tourist sites, and in markets and at fiestas. The rules are those you should follow anywhere. Don't leave valuables unattended, don't take them to the beach or leave them visible in a car. Make use of hotel safe-boxes where possible. Don't carry large sums of money or wear expensive jewellery, and keep hold of your camera. Be especially careful when getting money from automatic cash machines.

In Maó, report thefts and break-ins to the Policía Nacional; elsewhere, to the Guardia Civil.

I want to report a theft. **Quiero denunciar un robo.**

D

DRIVING

Menorca's highway between Maó and Ciutadella, the Me-1, is very good, but can get crowded in summer. Some other roads are narrow and poorly surfaced, but great improvements have been made in recent years. Road signs are not always as clear as they might be. Be aware that there is no road running all the way round the coast.

Rules and regulations. The rules are the same as throughout Spain: drive on the right, overtake on the left, yield to vehicles coming from the right (unless your road is marked as having priority). Seat belts are compulsory. Children up to the age of 12 and measuring less than 135cm must travel in an adequate child restraint. You should always carry your driving licence with you, as well as proof of insurance, and it is a good idea to have a photocopy of your passport. Speed limits are 120 km/h (75mph) on motorways and dual carriageways, 90–100km/h (56–62mph) on main roads, 50km/h (32mph) on minor roads and in the cities and 30km/h (18mph) on unpaved roads.

Traffic police. Roads are patrolled by the Guardia Civil de Tráfico on motorbikes. They are generally courteous and helpful, but are tough on lawbreakers. Fines are payable on the spot. Don't drink and drive. The permitted blood-alcohol level is low and penalties are stiff.

Fuel. There are 14 service stations on Menorca, several grouped around the two main cities. Lead-free petrol *(gasolina)* comes in grades 90 and 98. Diesel fuel is widely available. Fuel is slightly cheaper than in the UK but will seem expensive to US visitors.

Parking. Finding a place to park can be difficult in Maó and Ciutadella, but is not a problem elsewhere. Maó, Ciutadella and others have 'blue zone' metered areas, denoted by a blue 'P' and blue lines on the road. There are also some public car parks.

Mechanical problems. Garages are efficient, but repairs may take time

¿Se puede aparcar aquí? Can I park here?
Llénelo, por favor. Fill the tank please.
Ha habido un accidente. There has been an accident.

in busy tourist areas. For emergencies, call Spanish Real Automóvil Club (RACE; tel: 900 112 222; www.race.es) or the Catalan Automóvil Club (RACC; tel: 900 242 242; www.racc.es).

Road signs. Most signs are the standard pictographs found throughout Europe, but the words below may be useful.

> Aparcamiento **Parking**
> Desviación **Detour**
> Obras **Road works**
> Peatones **Pedestrians**
> Peligro **Danger**
> Senso único **One way**

E

ELECTRICITY

The 220-v system is standard. Sockets take round, two-pin plugs, so you will need an adapter, found in UK chemists, supermarkets and at airports. US visitors will need a transformer.

EMBASSIES AND CONSULATES

Canada: For minor matters contact the UK honorary consulate in Maó. In other cases, contact: Embassy of Canada to Spain in Madrid, Torre Espacio, Paseo de la Castellana 259 D, tel: 91 382 8400, www.canada international.gc.ca.

Ireland: (Honorary Consul) Carrer Sant Miquel 68, 8ª, Palma, tel: 971 719 244 or 971 722 504, www.dfa.ie.

UK: (Honorary Consul) Camí Biniatap 30, Es Castell, Maó, tel: 902 109 356.

US: Consulate General in Barcelona, Paseo Reina Elisenda de Montcada, Barcelona, tel: 93 280 22 27.

> Where is the British/American consulate? **¿Dónde está el consulado británico/americano?**

EMERGENCIES

General emergency number (police, fire, ambulance): 112
National Police: 091
Municipal Police: 092
Guardia Civil: 062
Ambulance: 061 and Fire: 080

> Police! **Policía!**
> Help! **Socorro!**
> Fire! **Fuego!**
> Stop! **Deténgase!**

G

GETTING THERE

Air travel. Menorca's airport is linked by regular scheduled flights with London, Berlin, Frankfurt and other European cities, but some of them, including Iberia, British Airways and Air Europa go via Barcelona, Madrid or Palma. Monarch flies direct from Gatwick, Luton, Birmingham and Manchester. From Dublin, flights go via Madrid or London. Flights from the US and Canada go via London or Madrid and then on to Palma. Flight time from the UK (direct) is about 2.5 hours. From Australia and New Zealand, you go via London to Madrid or Barcelona, then get a connecting flight.

For scheduled flights from the UK, contact Iberia (tel: 901 111 500, www.iberia.com), British Airways (tel: 0844-493 0787, www.britishairways.

com) or Monarch Airlines (tel: 0333-003 0700, www.monarch.co.uk). From Eire, contact Aer Lingus (tel: 1890 800 600, www.aerlingus.com), although there is no direct flight to Menorca. The website of Opodo (www.opodo.com) finds the best flights operated by a number of major airlines.

In the US and Canada, contact Iberia (tel: 1-800 772 4642, www.iberia.com) or British Airways (US tel: 1-800 452 1201, Canada tel: 1-800 247 9297, www.britishairways.com).

Easyjet (www.easyjet.com) flies from UK airports to Maó. There are also direct flights from Bristol, London Gatwick and London Luton, more frequent in summer and less frequent in other months. From December to February there are no direct flights at all. Flights on Air Nostrum (tel: 901 111 500, www.airnostrum.es, for booking go to Iberia's website) from Palma to Maó take 35 minutes and cost from €60 return. Other operators flying to Menorca include Thomas Cook (tel: 0871 2302406, flythomascook.com), Thomson (tel: 0871 2314787, thomsonfly.com) and Jet2 (tel: 0906 3020660, www.jet2.com).

By sea. The shipping company Balearia offers frequent connections between Mallorca and Menorca; ferries run between Port d'Alcúdia and Ciutadella (tel: 902 160 180, www.balearia.com). The journey takes about 2 hours. Trasmediterránea offers direct service between Palma de Mallorca and Maó that takes 5 hours (tel: 902 454 645, www.trasmediterranea.es). Both companies provide also car transport.

In summer there are daily direct links from Barcelona to Maó via Trasmediterránea, journey time about 9 hours; off-season the service runs three times a week. There's also a weekly service between Valencia and Maó, journey time about 15 hours. There is also a Baleària service between Barcelona and Ciutadella (about 9 hours).

H

HEALTH AND MEDICAL CARE

Standards of hygiene on Menorca are generally high; the most common problems visitors encounter are due to an excess of sun or alcohol. Bottled water is always safest, and is available everywhere. *Agua con gas* is carbonated water; *agua sin gas* is still.

There are doctors' surgeries in all towns: look for the Centro de Salud or Consultorio Local. For less serious matters, first-aid personnel *(called practicantes)* make daily rounds of the larger resort hotels. Many resorts have medical centres *(centros medicos)*, privately run institutions that must be paid on the spot, in cash or by credit card (roughly €50 per consultation). The private healthcare network Juaneda (tel: 971 731 647, www.juaneda.es) has clinics all over the island, and staff speak both English and German.

There is a good modern general hospital in Maó: Hospital Mateu Orfila, Ronda Malbúger 13, tel: 971 487 000, emergencies tel: 971 487 030, and the private Juaneda Mahón (Carrer Vives Llull 6, tel: 971 351 115). In Ciutadella there's the public Centro de Salud Canal Salat (Carrer Sant Antoni M. Claret, tel: 971 480 112) and the private Juaneda Menorca (Canonge Moll 1, tel: 971 480 505). All open 24 hours for emergencies.

It is always advisable to take out insurance to cover illness or accident. EU residents are entitled to reciprocal health arrangements on production of the European health insurance card (EHIC), available free in your home country, but it does not cover all eventualities.

Pharmacies *(farmácias)* are open during shopping hours, but there is at least one – the *farmácia de guardia* – open all night in Maó and Ciutadella. In smaller towns, it may be difficult to find an after-hours pharmacy. A list showing the pharmacy on rota duty is posted in chemists' windows. Spanish pharmacists are highly trained and generally

Where's the nearest (all-night) chemist? **¿Dónde está la farmácia (de guardia) más cercana?**
I need a doctor/dentist **Necesito un médico/dentista.**
sunburn/sunstroke **quemadura del sol/una insolación**
an upset stomach **molestias de estómago**

speak some English.

Emergency medical assistance can be obtained by contacting the Red Cross (Cruz Roja), www.cruzroja.es, tel: 112 or 971 361 180 (Maó), tel: 971 381 993 (Ciutadella).

HOLIDAYS

The following are official public holidays. There are a number of other regional holidays, usually saints' days, dotted throughout the year; tourist offices will tell you when the main ones are. Two major events are the *Festes de Sant Joan* in Ciutadella (St John' Day) celebrated on 23–24 June and *Festes de la Vierge de Gracia* in Maó on 7–9 September (see page 96).

1 January *Año Nuevo* New Year's Day
6 January *Epifanía* Epiphany
17 January *Día de Menorca* and *San Antonio* Menorca's and St Antony's Day
1 May *Día del Trabajo* Labour Day
15 August *Asunción* Assumption
12 October *Día de la Hispanidad* National Day
1 November *Todos los Santos* All Saints' Day
6 December *Día de la Constitución Española* Constitution Day
8 December *Inmaculada Concepción* Immaculate Conception
25 December *Navidad* Christmas Day
Movable dates:
Late March/April *Jueves Santo* Maundy Thursday
Late March/April *Viernes Santo* Good Friday
Late March/April *Lunes de Pascua* Easter Monday
Mid-June *Corpus Christi* Corpus Christi

L

LANGUAGE

While Castilian Spanish is the national language, a local form of Catalan – Menorquí – is now the official language of the island and is more widely spoken; however, almost all islanders speak both. Most street signs appear only in Catalan, although the names of some establishments often seem to be a mixture of the two languages and some older people still use the Spanish names. If you know some Spanish, you'll be fine; the effort to speak Catalan is appreciated, but it is not necessary. English and German are widely spoken in resort areas, and making oneself understood is rarely a problem.

The *Berlitz Spanish Phrasebook* covers most situations you're likely to encounter.

LGBTQ TRAVELLERS

The Balearics are among the most hospitable places in Spain for LGBTQ travellers. Contact Ben Amics, tel: 871 96 54 66, www.benamics.com.

> Do you speak English? **¿Habla usted inglés?**
> I don't speak Spanish. **No hablo español.**

M

MAPS

The map of the island produced by the tourist board and available at all tourist information offices should be sufficient, even for those travelling by car. Just make sure you are clear which are rough tracks and which asphalted roads, as the distinction on maps is not always as obvious as it might be. The tourist office in Maó provides excellent little maps of the two cities. A good place for more specific maps and books on the is-

> Do you have a map of the city/island? **¿Tiene un plano de la a ciudad/isla?**

land is La Católica library (Carrer Hannover 14, Maó; Mon–Fri 9.30am–1.30pm and 5–8pm, Sat 9.30am–2pm).

MEDIA

In main tourist areas most English and German newspapers are sold on the day of publication during the summer months. The Paris-based *International Herald Tribune* and the European edition of the *Wall Street Journal* are also available, as are the principal European and American magazines. For Spanish speakers, the *Diario de Menorca* (www.menorca.info) and all Spanish national papers and magazines are available.

Most hotels and bars have television, usually tuned to sports, and broadcasting in Castilian, Catalan and Menorquí. Satellite dishes are popular and most tourist hotels offer multiple channels (German, French, Sky, BBC, CNN, etc). Reception of Britain's BBC World Service radio is usually good. A good set will (sometimes) receive BBC long-wave and even medium-wave domestic programmes.

MONEY

Currency. Spain's monetary unit is the euro (€), which is divided into 100 cents. Bank notes are available in denominations of 5, 10, 20, 50, 100, 200 and 500 euros, and there are coins for 1 and 2 euros and for 1, 2, 5, 10, 20 and 50 cents.

Currency exchange. Banks are the most straightforward option. A large number of travel agencies exchange foreign currency, and *casas de cambio* (exchange offices) stay open outside banking hours. Be wary of those advertising 'no commission' – their rates are considerably lower than those offered elsewhere, so you are in effect paying a hefty commission. Always take your passport as proof of identity.

Credit cards. Major international credit cards are widely recognised, although smaller businesses tend to prefer cash. Visa/Eurocard/MasterCard are the most widely accepted. Credit and debit cards are also useful for obtaining cash from ATMs – cash machines – which are found in all towns and resorts. They offer the most convenient way of obtaining cash and will usually give you the best exchange rate.

> Where's the nearest bank/currency exchange office?
> **¿Dónde está el banco más cercano/la oficina de cambio más cercana?**
> I want to change some dollars/pounds. **Quiero cambiar dólares/libres esterlina.**
> Can I pay with this credit card?**¿Puedo pagar con esta tarjeta de crédito?**

O

OPENING TIMES

Shops and offices: 9.30am–1.30pm and 5–8pm. Large supermarkets and department stores usually open all day, and some until 10pm.

Museums and other attractions: the hours of the major museums are given in the relevant section of this guide. Many close on Monday, and also for a longish midday break.

Post offices: Monday to Friday 8.30am–2.30pm.

Banks: Monday–Sat 8.15am–2pm.

Restaurants: lunch from 1–3.30pm, dinner 8–11pm.

P

POLICE

Spanish municipal and national police *(policía)* are efficient, strict and courteous, and generally very responsive to issues involving tourists.

The general emergency number for all services is 112. Dial 092 for municipal police and 091 for national police. The municipal police station in Maó can be contacted on tel: 971 363 961, in Ciutadella, tel: 971 380 787.

POST OFFICES

Identified by yellow-and-white signs with a crown and the words *Correos y Telégrafos*, post offices are for mail and telegrams; you can't telephone from them. Check www.correos.es for information. The postal system is pretty reliable and efficient. Opening hours are usually Monday to Friday 8.30am–2.30pm and Saturday 9am–1pm. The main post office in Maó is on Carrer Bon Aire, tel: 971 356 629; in Ciutadella, it is in Plaça des Born, tel: 971 380 081. Stamps *(sellos)* are also sold by tobacconist's *(estancos/tabacos)* and by most shops selling postcards, although they do appreciate it if you buy your postcards there, too.

> Where is the (nearest) post office? **¿Dónde está la oficina de correos (más cercana)?**
> A stamp for this letter/postcard, please. **Por favor, un sello para esta carta/tarjeta.**

PUBLIC TRANSPORT

Bus (autobus). Regular bus services run from Maó and Ciutadella to most towns and resorts. The vehicles are clean and easy to use, fares are reasonable and drivers are generally friendly and helpful. Destinations are marked on the front of the buses. In Maó, most buses start from the terminal in Carrer Vassallo behind Plaça de s'Esplanada (ask for the *estación de autobuses*). Contact Transportes Menorca (TMSA), tel: 971 360 475, www.tmsa.es or https://menorca.tib.org for detailed information. In Ciutadella, most services commence at the terminal in Plaça des Pins (beside Plaça des Born). It is not so easy to travel between smaller towns by bus – you usually have to return to one of the two main terminals, which can make relatively short distances take quite a long time. To travel up to the north of the island you can also check Autos Fornells (tel: 971 154 390, www.autosfornells.com, only from 1 May until 31 October). The airport bus is run by a different company, Torres (tel: 971 384 720, www.e-torres.net).

Taxi. Taxi prices in Menorca compare favourably with those in many countries. Check the fare before you get in; rates are fixed and are displayed in several languages on the windows. Hotel reception staff will always book taxis for you, but a few useful phone numbers are: Maó: Radio Taxi (tel: 971 367 111/971 482 222, www.taximenorca.es), taxi stand in Plaça d'España (tel: 971 362 891), in Plaça de s'Esplanada (tel: 971 361 283). In Ciutadella, try: = Taxis 24h (tel: 971 482 222; www.taxis 24h.com), taxi stand in Avinguda Constitució (tel: 971 381 197), in Plaça d'es Born (tel: 971 384 435) and in Sant Lluis (tel: 971 150 641). It's also possible to book a taxi via email (taxi@taximenorca.es).

Train. There is no train service on the island.

T

TELEPHONES

Spain's country code is 34. The local area code, 971, must be dialled before all phone numbers, even for local calls.

The telephone office is independent of the post office and is identified by a blue-and-white sign. You can make direct-dial local and international calls from public telephone booths (cabinas) in the street. Some accept both coins and cards but card-only phones are more prevalent; international phone cards and credit cards can also be used. You can buy a phone card (tarjeta telefónica) in various denominations at any estanco (tobacconist's shop). Instructions for use are given in several languages in the booths. In Maó, Ciutadella and some of the bigger resorts you can also use public telephone offices called locutorios. This is quieter than making a call on the street, and more convenient, as you pay afterwards. To make an international call, dial 00, then the country code plus the phone number, omitting any initial zero. Calls are cheapest after 10pm on weekdays, after 2pm on Saturday, and all day Sunday.

Note that as of June 2017, there are no roaming charges within the EU.

TIME ZONES

The Balearics keep the same time as mainland Spain, which is one hour ahead of GMT. Spanish time is hence generally one hour ahead of London, the same as Paris and six hours ahead of New York.

TIPPING

A service charge is sometimes included on restaurant bills (look for the words *servicio incluido*). If not, it is usual to tip waiters 10 percent and taxi drivers a similar amount; it's normal to leave a few coins, rounding up the bill, at a bar counter. Porters, hairdressers and chambermaids should be given €1–2.

TOILETS

There are many expressions for toilets in Spanish: *servicios, aseos* or *lavabos* are the most commonly used. Toilet doors usually have a 'C' for Caballeros (Gentlemen), or an 'S' for Señoras (Ladies). Public toilets exist in some large towns but they are rare; most bars will allow you to use their facilities without asking if you are a customer. Those that object usually keep the key behind the bar so you have to ask for it.

TOURIST INFORMATION OFFICES

Before leaving, you can get information from the Spanish Tourist Office in your home country:

Canada: 2 Bloor Street West, Suite 3402, Toronto, Ontario M4W 3E2, tel: 1416-961 3131.

UK: 64 North Row, Sixth floor, London W1K 7DE, visits by previous appointment only, tel: 020 7317 2011, information line tel: 0870-850 6599, www.spain.info/en_GB.

US: Water Tower Place, Suite 915 East, 845 North Michigan Avenue, Chicago, IL 60611, tel: 312-642 1992.

8383 Wilshire Boulevard, Suite 960, Beverly Hills, CA 90211, tel: 213-658 7188.

60 East 42nd Street, Suite 5300, New York, NY 10103, tel: 212-265 8822.

Tourist offices in Menorca

There is a multilingual, island-wide tourist information line, tel: 902 929 015. The main tourist offices are:

Maó: Plaça Constitució 22, Maó, tel: 971 363 790, email: infomenorca mao@menorca.es.

Port de Maó, Moll de Levant 2, tel: 971 355 952, email: infomenorca-port@menorca.es.

Aeroport de Maó, Arrivals Hall, tel: 971 157 115, email: infomenorca eroport@menorca.es.

Ciutadella: Plaça de's Born (town hall), tel: 971 484 155, infomenorca ciutadella@menorca.es.

There are offices in many other resorts and towns, although they are usually only open in summer. Staff are usually helpful and speak some English or German. They may have lists of hotels but do not as a rule assist with finding accommodation.

TRAVELLERS WITH DISABILITIES

The Balearic Islands, like mainland Spain, are becoming increasingly geared up to receiving visitors with disabilities these days. Maó airport and most large modern hotels have wheelchair access and facilities for travellers with disabilities, although visiting some churches and museums/galleries and negotiating narrow streets may present more of a problem. For general information, consult the online *Able Magazine*, 36–38 Washington Street, Glasgow G3 8AZ, tel: 0141 285 4000, www.ablemagazine.co.uk.

Tourism for All (tel: 0845 124 9974 or international tel: 044 1293 776 225 (overseas), www.tourismforall.org.uk) also provides information for travellers with disabilities.

V

VISAS AND ENTRY REQUIREMENTS

Citizens of the UK, the US, Canada, Australia and New Zealand need only a valid passport to enter Spain and the Balearics, for a stay of up to 90 days. Citizens of South Africa need a visa. Full information on passport and visa regulations is available from the Spanish Embassy in your own country.

As Spain is part of the European Union (EU), free exchange of non-duty-free items for personal use is permitted between Spain and other EU countries. However, duty-free items are still subject to restrictions. There are no limits on the amount of money that you may import, but you should declare sums over the equivalent of €10,000.

W

WEBSITES AND INTERNET ACCESS

www.illesbalears.es useful site for general information, museums, outdoor activities and much more

http://menorca.costasur.com general information including accommodation, transport and useful phone numbers

www.menorca.es the official tourist website of the island, provided by local authority Consell Insular de Menorca

www.visitmenorca.com Menorca Hotel Association site

http://balearsculturaltour.net Balearic Islands culture, gastronomy and history provided by the Balearic tourist office

www.illesbalearsqualitat.es lowdown on the best products of the Balearic Islands

www.biosferamenorca.org nature and environment protection website

There is free Wi-fi on the main squares, as well as in most bars and cafés (ask for the password) across the island. There are a dwindling number of internet cafés in Maó, Ciutadella and the main resorts.

RECOMMENDED HOTELS

There is a wide range of accommodation available on Menorca, from luxury hotels to small, family-run hostels, as well as the huge, impersonal, but efficient modern hotels in the resorts, where much of the accommodation is block-booked by tour companies. Officially, establishments are classified as *pensiónes*, *hostales* or *hoteles*, but the lines between them are often blurred. Prices drop considerably out of season, but many hotels close between November and Easter, so the cheaper periods are usually from mid-April to mid-June and mid-September to the end of October. Finding winter accommodation isn't always easy and places that stay open all year will be indicated in the listings below. For details on rural *(agroturismo)* holidays, see www.menorcaturismorural.net. Alternatively, go to www.toprural.com.

A growing number of establishments include a buffet breakfast in the quoted price; some rates also include IVA, the 10 percent value-added tax on hotel rooms, but it is not standard, so it is wise to check. Web addresses are given only when they are specific to the hotel, rather than reservation agencies. In the listings, the following ranges are used to indicate prices for a double room per night in high season and are given as a guide only:

€€€€	over 250 euros
€€€	125–250 euros
€€	75–125 euros
€	below 75 euros

MAÓ AND ES CASTELL

Almirante €€ *Carretera Maó–Es Castell, tel: 971 362 700*, www.hoteldelalmirante.com. A friendly, somewhat old-fashioned hotel in a Georgian mansion built for Nelson's right-hand man, Lord Collingwood. There are 10 antique-furnished bedrooms and a lounge in the main hotel, and 29 other rooms built hacienda-style around a garden and pool. There's a tennis court, billiard room and massage facilities. Situated half way between Maó and Es Castell. Special terms for regular guests, of whom there are many.

Barceló Hamilton €€€ *Passeig Santa Agueda 6, Es Castell, tel: 971 362 050*, www.barcelo.com. This big renovated hotel has 160 rooms, most with sea views; there is also a pool and a buffet restaurant. Its bold design and state-of-the art features make it a good choice for couples and business travellers. Wellness and fitness facilities are available. Open all year. Adults only.

Capri €€ *Carrer Sant Esteve 8, tel: 971 361 400*, www.artiemhotels.com/en/capri-en/capri-location. Modern, efficient and comfortable, if somewhat characterless, the Capri, part of the Artiem chain, is close to the Plaça de s'Esplanada. The glass-enclosed pool and jacuzzi have views over the city. This hotel caters to pre-booked groups. Open all year.

Hostal Jume € *Carrer Concepció 6, tel: 971 363 266*, www.hostaljume.com. In a large, modern block near Plaça de Miranda, the Jume offers basic rooms with bathrooms at a modest price. Breakfast is available. Credit cards accepted. Closed Christmas period.

La Isla € *Carrer Santa Catalina 4, tel: 971 366 492*, www.hostal-laisla.com/en/. A basic but friendly *hostal* in a narrow street to the east of the centre. All 22 rooms are en suite and have televisions. There's also a bar and restaurant downstairs. Closed mid-Dec–mid-Jan.

Port Mahón €€€ *Avinguda Port de Maó s/n, tel: 971 362 600*, www.sethotels.com/en/port-mahon-hotel-en.html. A splendid rusty-red colonial-style mansion overlooking the harbour, about 15 minutes' walk from the centre. Comfortable, air-conditioned rooms, most with balconies; excellent service, pool, terrace bar, restaurant and lovely gardens. Open all year.

Posada Orsi € *Carretera Infanta 19, tel: 971 364 751*, www.posadaorsi.es. Centrally located, this small, simple and efficient *hostal* occupies a typical Menorcan house. Rooms are decorated with attractive ethnic touches and there is a brightly coloured 'chill-out room'. One room has a roof terrace with an amazing view. Some rooms have their own bathrooms, while others are shared.

CIUTADELLA AND ENVIRONS

Globales Almirante Farragut €€€ *Cala en Forcat, tel: 971 388 000*, www.hotelesglobales.com. Right by the sea, the hotel offers comfortable air-conditioned rooms, an outdoor pool and a tennis court. Two nights minimum stay required.

Ciutadella €€ *Carrer Sant Eloi 10, tel: 971 383 462*, www.hostalciutadella.com. Located close to the Plaça de Ses Palmeras this modest but comfortable little place is good value and has its own restaurant. Open all year.

Hotel Menorca Patricia €€ *Passeig Sant Nicolau 90–2, tel: 971 385 511*, www.hotelmenorcapatricia.com. A modern, comfortable and well-appointed hotel in a quiet street close to the port and only a few minutes' walk from Plaça d'es Born. Business centre and conference facilities. The restaurant (breakfast and lunch only) is recommended. Small pool.

Hotel Rural Biniatram €€€ *Carretera Cala Morell, tel: 971 383 113*, www.biniatram.com. This is a traditional Menorcan *finca*, whose origins go back 500 years. In peaceful countryside just outside Cala Morell, only 7km (4 miles) from Ciutadella, the hotel is set in beautiful gardens. Amenities include a large pool and tennis court. Breakfast not included in the price. Also rents apartments.

Hotel Rural Sant Ignasi €€€–€€€€ *Carretera Cala Morell, tel: 971 385 575*, www.santignasi.com. This 18th-century manor house, set in farmland 4km (2.5 miles) north of Ciutadella, manages to be both rustic and elegant. Each room is different – all are furnished with antiques, while some have huge terraces. There's an excellent restaurant and an inviting bar and pool. Closed mid-Dec–mid-Jan.

Madrid € *Carrer Madrid 60, tel: 971 380 328*, www.hotelmadridmenorca.com. In a quiet street 10 minutes' walk from Plaça d'es Born, this little hostel is basic and friendly. All 22 rooms are en suite and have balconies, some with harbour views. There's a bar, cafeteria and a small pool – although the pool is right by the road.

Morvedra Nou €€€ *Camí de Sant Joan de Missa Km 7, tel: 971 359 521*, www.morvedranou.es. A 17th-century house offers comfortable accommodation in a rural atmosphere. Set in peaceful countryside with splendid views, only 7km (4 miles) from Ciutadella and about the same from the beaches of Cala Turqueta and Cala Macarella. Pool and gardens. Horse-riding excursions can be organised.

Port Ciutadella €€€ *Passeig Marítim 36, tel: 971 482 520*, www.sethotels.com. A luxurious hotel close to Platja Gran, with 94 rooms, including 18 suites furnished in minimalist style. Pool, spa, gym and conference facilities. Four rooms adapted for wheelchair users.

Sa Prensa € *Carrer Madrid 70, tel: 971 382 698*, www.saprensa.com. Sa Prensa is an unpretentious and functional *hostal* on the next block from the Madrid. The eight double rooms are all en suite and some have balconies with sea views. There is a café and bar on the ground floor.

Tres Sants €€€ *Carrer Sant Cristofol 2, tel: 626 053 536*, www.grupel carme.com. Located in the heart of the old town, this 18th-century manor house has eight rooms, each one with unique decor, Turkish baths and a swimming pool in the basement. Spectacular views from the rooftop terrace. No parking available.

THE NORTHEAST

Fornells

El Bergantin Menorca Club € *Carrer Es Tamarells s/n, Platges de Fornells, tel: 971 376 506*, www.elbergantinmenorca.com. This family-owned hotel is located just 3km (2 miles) from Fornells. It offers apartments and studios with bathroom, kitchenette and beautiful sea-view balcony. There is also a swimming pool and a snack bar. A perfect base for exploring the island.

Hostal La Palma €€ *Plaça S'Algaret 3, tel: 971 376 634*, www.hostalla palma.com. Right by the harbour, this friendly place has simply furnished rooms, some overlooking the sea, others with views of the garden and small pool. There's a busy local bar on the ground floor. Apartments are available for rent in winter, when the hotel is otherwise closed.

Hostal Residencia Port Fornells €€ *Urbanización Ses Salines, tel: 971 376 373*, www.hostalportfornells.com. The location on the lagoon in the Ses Salines development, just south of town, makes this easy-going place popular with windsurfers.

Hostal S'Algaret €€ *Plaça S'Algaret 7, tel: 971 376 552/971 376 499*, www.hostal-salgaret.com. This hotel offers functional, plain and pleasant rooms, as well as a small pool. There are harbour views from the first-floor restaurant's floor-to-ceiling windows and rooms have small terraces with garden/pool views.

THE SOUTH

Binibeca Vell

ATH Binivell Parc €€ *Complejo Binibeca Vell, tel: 971 150 412*. There are apartments and studios to rent in this twee but pretty architect-designed 'fishermen's village' with swimming pools, restaurants, bars and shops.

Cala Blanca

Cala Blanca Sun Hotel €€€ *Urbanizacion Cala Blanca 11–13, tel: 971 38 04 50*. A large four-star hotel close to Macarelleta Beach and Naveta d'Es Tudons, as well as central Ciutadella. It boasts 163 air-conditioned rooms with balconies and satellite TV, two outdoor pools (one for children), a restaurant and bar, plus free Wi-fi. It was thoroughly renovated in 2015. Closed Oct–mid-May.

Globales Hotel Mediterrani €€ *Urbanización Cala Blanca, tel: 971 384 203*, www.hotelesglobales.com. The hotel is high-rise, modern and not very beautiful; however, the 180 air-conditioned rooms are comfortable and have large balconies, the service is good and the hotel is very close to the beach. It is mostly booked by tour groups but some rooms are available for individual travellers.

Cala en Bosc

La Quinta €€€€ *Gran Vía de Son Xoriguer, tel: 971 055 000*, www.portblue hotels.com. A five-star spa hotel in a colonial-style building, furnished with traditional materials, close to the beaches of Son Xoriguer and Cala en Bosc. As well as a large outdoor pool, it has a heated indoor pool and Turkish bath and offers water massage treatments. A place to go if you want to be pampered.

Cala N'Porter

Castillo Sancho Panza € *Avenida Central 75, tel: 971 377 868*, www.hostal castillosanchopanza.com. This very quirky *hostal* built as a medieval castle has 8 air-conditioned rooms, all equipped with bathrooms and Wi-fi. Half-board accommodation is available. Good value for money.

Cala Santa Galdana

Cala Galdana and Villas d'Aljandar €€€ *Urbanización Serpentona, tel: 971 154 500*, www.hotelcalagaldana.com. A large, efficient, international-style hotel on the road paralleling the river. Caters largely to tour groups but does have rooms for individual guests. Live entertainment, gym, children's playground and four restaurants. Minimum three-night stay in high season. Also has an attractive apartment-bungalow complex.

Rtm Audax Spa & Wellness Centre €€€ *Urbanización Serpentona, tel: 971 154 646*, www.artiemhotels.com/en/audax-hotel. A large, modern hotel, the Audax has 244 air-conditioned rooms with balconies and views of either the sea, the pool or pine woods. Facilities include a gym, sauna, jacuzzi and hair salon. The hotel can organise all kinds of outdoor activities, from canoeing to hiking and archery.

Sol Gavilanes €€€ *Cala Santa Galdana, tel: 971 154 545*, www.melia.com. A massive pile dominating the bay. Its own views are splendid, even if they rather spoil other people's. It is a comfortable place to stay and the service is efficient; there are three restaurants, two pools and sports facilities.

Sant Lluís

Biniarroca Hotel Rural €€€ *Camí Vell, Carretera Sant Lluís–Es Castell, tel: 971 150 059*, www.biniarroca.com. This 15th-century farmhouse has been lovingly converted into an elegant country hotel. The rooms have period furniture, and oil paintings on the walls. There are peaceful gardens, an attractive pool and an award-winning restaurant. Offers special deals in April, May and June.

Binissafullet Vell €€€ *Carretera Binissafullet 64, tel: 971 150 722*, www.binissafullet.com. An attractive rural *agroturismo* property set in leafy gardens with a small pool. Eight well-furnished rooms with beamed ceilings. Open all year.

Hotel S'Algar €€€ *Avenida Tercera, S'Algar, tel: 971 151 700*, www.salgar hotels.com. An attractive spot with whitewashed arched buildings, a large pool, a spa, sea views and lovely gardens. Contains 106 rooms with terraces. Free Wi-fi in public areas.

Sant Tomàs

Hotel 55 Santo Tomàs €€€ *Carrer Playa Santo Tomás, tel: 971 355 822*, www.sethotels.com. Very close to the beach, this modern, streamlined hotel has 165 air-conditioned rooms, each with a small balcony or terrace. There is an indoor heated pool for cooler days.

Son Bou

Hotel Valentín Son Bou €€ *Urbanización Torresolí Nou, tel: 902 585 265*, www.valentinhotels.com. The low-rise four-star Hotel Valentín is set on a slight hill above the resort of Son Bou, surrounded by pine trees. It's a family-friendly place with helpful staff. Apartments are also available for self-catering. There is a six-night minimum stay in high season.

Sol Pinguinos Milanos €€ *Platja Son Bou, tel: 971 371 200*, www.melia.com/en/hotels/spain/menorca/sol-milanos-pinguinos/index.html. A monolithic monster right by the beach. The rooms of these two adjoining hotels have balconies and there are all the modern conveniences and facilities you would expect from such an immense complex.

THE CENTRE

Es Mercadal

Es Mercadal €€ *Carrer Nou 49, tel: 971 154 439*, www.hotelesmercadal. com. Located on the main street of Es Mercadal, this typical Menorcan house, built by the end of the 19th century, has six charming rooms, each one with unique decor. The hotel offers horse and boat excursions on the north coast as well as transport to and from the airport.

Hostal Jeni €€ *Carrer Mirador del Toro 81, tel: 971 375 059*, www.hostaljeni. com. In a big ochre-coloured building at the east end of the town is this simple but very pleasant *hostal*. There's a heated pool with a retractable roof and a good restaurant serving imaginative *cuina menorquina*. Recent renovation has equipped the hotel with facilities for people with disabilities. Two-night minimum stay in high season.

Es Migjorn Gran

S'Engolidor €€ *Carrer Major 3, tel: 971 370193*, www.sengolidor.es. Five delightfully old-fashioned en-suite rooms in an 18th-century house, furnished with antiques and knick-knacks. There is no name outside to tell you that this is a hotel – just look for the house number. S'Engolidor also has a splendid and well-known restaurant serving Menorcan dishes in a delightful dining room or on an outside terrace (see page 113).

Ferreries

Son Triay Nou €€ *Carretera Santa Galdana Km 2.5, tel: 971 155 078*, www. sontriay.com. This distinctive pink colonial-style building, about 3km (2 miles) from Ferreries and 4km (3 miles) from Cala Santa Galdana, is a friendly and relaxing place to stay, and makes a good starting point for walks nearby. Set in extensive grounds, it has a pool and tennis court. There are just eight attractively furnished rooms and six apartments.

DICTIONARY

ENGLISH–SPANISH

adj adjective   **adv** adverb   **BE** British English   **n** noun   **prep** preposition   **v** verb

A

abbey la abadía
accept v aceptar
access el acceso
accident el accidente
accommodation el alojamiento
account la cuenta
acupuncture la acupuntura
adapter el adaptador
address la dirección
admission la entrada
after después;
  ~noon la tarde;
  ~shave el bálsamo para después del afeitado
age la edad
agency la agencia
AIDS el sida
air el aire; ~
  conditioning el aire acondicionado;
  ~ pump el aire;
  ~line la compañía aérea; **~mail** el correo aéreo; **~plane** el avión; **~port** el aeropuerto
aisle el pasillo; ~ **seat** el asiento de pasillo
allergic alérgico; ~
  reaction la reacción alérgica

allow v permitir
alone solo
alter v (clothing) hacer un arreglo
alternate route el otro camino
aluminum foil el papel de aluminio
amazing increíble
ambulance la ambulancia
American estadounidense
amusement park el parque de atracciones
anemic anémico
anesthesia la anestesia
animal el animal
ankle el tobillo
antibiotic el antibiótico
antiques store la tienda de -antigüedades
antiseptic cream la crema antiséptica
anything algo
apartment el apartamento
appendix (body part) el apéndice
appetizer el aperitivo
appointment la cita
arcade el salón de juegos recreativos

area code el prefijo
arm el brazo
aromatherapy la aromaterapia
around (the corner) doblando (la esquina)
arrivals (airport) las llegadas
arrive v llegar
artery la arteria
arthritis la artritis
arts las letras
Asian asiático
aspirin la aspirina
asthmatic asmático
ATM el cajero automático
attack el asalto
attend v asistir
attraction (place) el sitio de interés
attractive guapo
Australia Australia
Australian australiano
automatic automático;
  ~ car coche automático
available disponible

B

baby el bebé; ~
  bottle el biberón;
  ~ wipe la toallita;
  ~sitter el/la canguro
back la espalda;

  ~ache el dolor de espalda; **~pack** la mochila
bag la maleta
baggage el equipaje;
  ~ claim la recogida de equipajes; **~ ticket** el talón de equipaje
bakery la panadería
ballet el ballet
bandage la tirita
bank el banco
bar el bar
barbecue la barbacoa
barber la peluquería de caballeros
baseball el béisbol
basket (grocery store) la cesta
basketball el baloncesto
bathroom el baño
battery (car) la batería
battery la pila
battleground el campo de batalla
be v ser, estar
beach la playa
beautiful precioso
bed la cama; ~ **and breakfast** la pensión
begin v empezar
before antes de

beginner principiante

behind detrás de

beige beis

belt el cinturón

berth la litera

best el/la mejor

better mejor

bicycle la bicicleta

big grande

bigger más grande

bike route el sendero para bicicletas

bikini el biquini; **~ wax** la depilación de las ingles

bill v **(charge)** cobrar; **~** n **(money)** el billete; **~** n **(of sale)** el recibo

bird el pájaro

birthday el cumpleaños

black negro

bladder la vejiga

bland soso

blanket la manta

bleed v sangrar

blood la sangre; **~ pressure** la tensión arterial

blouse la blusa

blue azul

board v embarcar

boarding pass la tarjeta de embarque

boat el barco

bone el hueso

book el libro; **~store** la librería

boots las botas

boring aburrido

botanical garden el jardín botánico

bother v molestar

bottle la botella; **~ opener** el abrebotellas

bowl el cuenco

box la caja

boxing match la pelea de boxeo

boy el niño; **~friend** el novio

bra el sujetador

bracelet la pulsera

brakes (car) los frenos

break v romper

break-in (burglary) el allanamiento de morada

breakdown la avería

breakfast el desayuno

breast el seno; **~feed** dar el pecho

breathe v respirar

bridge el puente

briefs (clothing) los calzoncillos

bring v traer

British británico

broken roto

brooch el broche

broom la escoba

brother el hermano

brown marrón

bug el insecto

building el edificio

burn v **(CD)** grabar

bus el autobús; **~ station** la estación de autobuses; **~ stop** la parada de autobús; **~ ticket** el billete de autobús; **~ tour** el recorrido en autobús

business los negocios; **~ card** la tarjeta de negocios; **~ cent-** er el centro de negocios; **~ class** la clase preferente; **~ hours** el horario de atención al público

butcher el carnicero

buttocks las nalgas

buy v comprar

bye adiós

C

cabaret el cabaré

cabin (house) la cabaña; **~ (ship)** el camarote

cable car el teleférico

cafe la cafetería

call v llamar; **~** n la llamada

calories las calorías

camera la cámara; **digital ~** la cámara digital; **~ case** la funda para la cámara; **~ store** la tienda de fotografía

camp v acampar; **~ stove** el hornillo; **~site** el cámping

can opener el abrelatas

Canada Canadá

Canadian canadiense

cancel v cancelar

candy el caramelo

canned goods las conservas

canyon el cañón

car el coche; **~ hire [BE]** el alquiler de coches; **~ park [BE]** el aparcamiento; **~ rental** el alquiler de coches; **~ seat** el asiento de niño

carafe la garrafa

card la tarjeta; **ATM ~** la tarjeta de cajero automático; **credit ~** la tarjeta de crédito; **debit ~** la tarjeta de débito; **phone ~** la tarjeta telefónica

carry-on (piece of hand luggage) el equipaje de mano

cart (grocery store) el carrito; **~ (luggage)** el carrito para el equipaje

carton el cartón; **~ of cigarettes** el cartón de tabaco

case (amount) la caja

cash v cobrar; **~** n el efectivo; **~ advance** sacar dinero de la tarjeta

cashier el cajero

casino el casino

castle el castillo

cathedral la catedral

cave la cueva

CD el CD

cell phone el teléfono móvil

Celsius el grado centígrado

centimeter el centímetro

certificate el certificado

chair la silla; **~ lift** la telesilla

change v **(buses)** cambiar; **~** n **(money)** el cambio

charcoal el carbón

charge v (credit card) cobrar; ~ n (cost) el precio

cheap barato

cheaper más barato

check v (on something) revisar; ~ v (luggage) facturar; ~ n (payment) el cheque; ~-in (airport) la facturación; ~-in (hotel) el registro; ~-out (hotel) la salida

Cheers! ¡Salud!

chemical toilet el váter químico

chemist [BE] la farmacia

cheque [BE] el cheque

chest (body part) el pecho; ~ pain el dolor de pecho

chewing gum el chicle

child el niño; ~ seat la silla para niños

children's menu el menú para niños

children's portion la ración para niños

Chinese chino

chopsticks los palillos chinos

church la iglesia

cigar el puro

cigarette el cigarrillo

class la clase; **business ~** la clase preferente; **economy ~** la clase económica; **first ~** la primera clase

classical music la música clásica

clean v limpiar; ~ adj limpio; **~ing product** el producto de limpieza; **~ing supplies** los productos de limpieza

clear v (on an ATM) borrar

cliff el acantilado

cling film [BE] el film transparente

close v (a shop) cerrar

closed cerrado

clothing la ropa; ~ **store** la tienda de ropa

club la discoteca

coat el abrigo

coffee shop la cafetería

coin la moneda

colander el escurridor

cold n (sickness) el catarro; ~ adj (temperature) frío

colleague el compañero de trabajo

cologne la colonia

color el color

comb el peine

come v venir

complaint la queja

computer el ordenador

concert el concierto; ~ **hall** la sala de conciertos

condition (medical) el estado de salud

conditioner el suavizante

condom el preservativo

conference la conferencia

confirm v confirmar

congestion la congestión

connect v (internet) conectarse

connection (internet) la conexión; ~ (flight) la conexión de vuelo

constipated estreñido

consulate el consulado

consultant el consultor

contact v ponerse en contacto con

contact lens la lentilla de contacto; ~ **solution** el líquido de lentillas de contacto

contagious contagioso

convention hall el salón de congresos

conveyor belt la cinta transportadora

cook v cocinar

cooking gas el gas butano

cool (temperature) frío

copper el cobre

corkscrew el sacacorchos

cost v costar

cot el catre

cotton el algodón

cough v toser; ~ n la tos

country code el código de país

cover charge la entrada

crash v (car) estrellarse

cream (ointment) la pomada

credit card la tarjeta de crédito

crew neck el cuello redondo

crib la cuna

crystal el cristal

cup la taza

currency la moneda; ~ **exchange** el cambio de divisas; ~ **exchange office** la casa de cambio

current account [BE] la cuenta corriente

customs las aduanas

cut v (hair) cortar; ~ n (injury) el corte

cute mono

cycling el ciclismo

D

damage v causar daño

damaged ha sufrido daños

dance v bailar; ~ **club** la discoteca

dangerous peligroso

dark oscuro

date (calendar) la fecha

day el día

deaf sordo

debit card la tarjeta de débito

deck chair la tumbona

declare v declarar

decline v (credit card) rechazar

deeply hondo

degrees (temperature) los grados

delay v retrasarse

delete v (computer) borrar
delicatessen la charcutería
delicious delicioso
denim tela vaquero
dentist el dentista
denture la dentadura
deodorant el desodorante
department store los grandes almacenes
departures (airport) las salidas
deposit v depositar; ~ n (bank) el depósito bancario; ~ v (reserve a room) la fianza
desert el desierto
dessert el postre
detergent el detergente
develop v (film) revelar
diabetic diabético
dial v marcar
diamond el diamante
diaper el pañal
diarrhea la diarrea
diesel el diesel
difficult difícil
digital digital; ~ **camera** la cámara digital; ~ **photos** las fotos digitales; ~ **prints** las fotos digitales
dining room el comedor
dinner la cena
direction la dirección
dirty sucio
disabled discapacitado; ~ **accessible**

[BE] el acceso para discapacitados
discharge (bodily fluid) la secreción
disconnect (computer) desconectar
discount el descuento
dish (kitchen) el plato; ~**washer** el lavavajillas; ~**washing liquid** el líquido lavavajillas
display v mostrar; ~ **case** la vitrina
disposable desechable; ~ **razor** la cuchilla desechable
dive v bucear
diving equipment el equipo de buceo
divorce v divorciar
dizzy mareado
doctor el médico
doll la muñeca
dollar (U.S.) el dólar
domestic nacional; ~ **flight** el vuelo nacional
door la puerta
dormitory el dormitorio
double bed la cama de matrimonio
downtown el centro
dozen la docena
drag lift el telesquí
dress (piece of clothing) el vestido; ~ **code** las normas de vestuario
drink v beber; ~ n la bebida, ~ **menu** la carta de bebidas;

~**ing water** el agua potable
drive v conducir
driver's license number el número de permiso de conducir
drop (medicine) la gota
drowsiness la somnolencia
dry cleaner la tintorería
dubbed doblada
during durante
duty (tax) el impuesto; ~**-free** libre de impuestos
DVD el DVD

E

ear la oreja; ~**ache** el dolor de oído
earlier más temprano
early temprano
earrings los pendientes
east el este
easy fácil
eat v comer
economy class la clase económica
elbow el codo
electric outlet el enchufe eléctrico
elevator el ascensor
e-mail v enviar un correo electrónico; ~ n el correo electrónico; ~ **address** la dirección de correo electrónico
emergency la emergencia; ~ **exit** la salida de urgencia

empty v vaciar
enamel (jewelry) el esmalte
end v terminar
English el inglés
engrave v grabar
enjoy v disfrutar
enter v entrar
entertainment el entretenimiento
entrance la entrada
envelope el sobre
equipment el equipo
escalators las escaleras mecánicas
e-ticket el billete electrónico
EU resident el/la residente de la UE
euro el euro
evening la noche
excess el exceso
exchange v (money) cambiar; ~ v (goods) devolver; ~ n (place) la casa de cambio; ~ **rate** el tipo de cambio
excursion la excursión
excuse v (to get past) pedir perdón; ~ v (to get attention) disculparse
exhausted agotado
exit v salir; ~ n la salida
expensive caro
expert (skill level) experto
exposure (film) la foto
express rápido; ~ **bus** el autobús rápido; ~ **train** el tren rápido

extension (phone) la extensión

extra adicional; **~ large** equis ele (XL)

extract v **(tooth)** extraer

eye el ojo

eyebrow wax la depilación de cejas

F

face la cara

facial la limpieza de cutis

family la familia

fan (appliance) el ventilador; **~ (souvenir)** el abanico

far lejos; **~-sighted** hipermétrope

farm la granja

fast rápido; **~ food** la comida rápida

faster más rápido

fat free sin grasa

father el padre

fax v enviar un fax; **~** n el fax; **~ number** el número de fax

fee la tasa

feed v alimentar

ferry el ferry

fever la fiebre

field (sports) el campo

fill v llenar ; **~ out** v **(form)** rellenar

filling (tooth) el empaste

film (camera) el carrete

fine (fee for breaking law) la multa

finger el dedo; **~nail** la uña del dedo

fire fuego; **~ department** los bomberos; **~ door** la puerta de incendios

first primero; **~ class** la primera clase

fit (clothing) quedar bien

fitting room el probador

fix v **(repair)** reparar

flashlight la linterna

flight el vuelo

floor el suelo

flower la flor

folk music la música folk

food la comida

foot el pie

football [BE] el fútbol

for para/por

forecast el pronóstico

forest el bosque

fork el tenedor

form el formulario

formula (baby) la fórmula infantil

fort el fuerte

fountain la fuente

free gratuito

freezer el congelador

fresh fresco

friend el amigo

frying pan la sartén

full completo; **~-service** el servicio completo; **~-time** a tiempo completo

G

game el partido

garage (parking) el garaje; **~ (repair)** el taller

garbage bag la bolsa de basura

gas la gasolina; **~ station** la gasolinera

gate (airport) la puerta

gay gay; **~ bar** el bar gay; **~ club** la discoteca gay

gel (hair) la gomina

get to v ir a

get off v **(a train/bus/subway)** bajarse

gift el regalo; **~ shop** la tienda de regalos

girl la niña; **~friend** la novia

give v dar

glass (drinking) el vaso; **~ (material)** el vidrio

glasses las gafas

go v **(somewhere)** ir a

gold el oro

golf golf; **~ course** el campo de golf; **~ tournament** el torneo de golf

good n el producto; **~** adj bueno; **~ afternoon** buenas tardes; **~ evening** buenas noches; **~ morning** buenos días; **~bye** adiós

gram el gramo

grandchild el nieto

grandparent el abuelo

gray gris

green verde

grocery store el supermercado

ground la tierra; **~ floor** la planta baja; **~cloth** la tela impermeable

group el grupo

guide el guía; **~ book** la guía; **~ dog** el perro guía

gym el gimnasio

gynecologist el ginecólogo

H

hair el pelo; **~ dryer** el secador de pelo; **~ salon** la peluquería; **~brush** el cepillo de pelo; **~cut** el corte de pelo; **~spray** la laca; **~style** el peinado; **~stylist** el estilista

half medio; **~ hour** la media hora; **~-kilo** el medio kilo

hammer el martillo

hand la mano; **~ luggage [BE]** el equipaje de mano; **~bag [BE]** el bolso

handicapped discapacitado; **~-accessible** el acceso para discapacitados

hangover la resaca

happy feliz

hat el sombrero

have v tener

head (body part) la cabeza; **~ache** el dolor de cabeza; **~phones** los cascos
health la salud; **~ food store** la tienda de alimentos naturales
heart el corazón; **~ condition** padecer del corazón
heat v calentar; **~** n el calor
heater [heating BE] la calefacción
hello hola
helmet el casco
help v ayudar; **~** n la ayuda
here aquí
hi hola
high alto; **~chair** la trona; **~way** la autopista
hiking boots las botas de montaña
hill la colina
hire v [BE] alquilar; **~ car** [BE] el coche de alquiler
hitchhike v hacer autostop
hockey el hockey
holiday [BE] las vacaciones
horse track el hipódromo
hospital el hospital
hostel el albergue
hot (temperature) caliente; **~ (spicy)** picante; **~ spring** el agua termale; **~ water** el

agua caliente
hotel el hotel
hour la hora
house la casa; **~hold goods** los artículos para el hogar; **~keeping services** el servicio de limpieza de habitaciones
how (question) cómo; **~ much (question)** cuánto cuesta
hug v abrazar
hungry hambriento
hurt v **(have pain)** tener dolor
husband el marido

I

ibuprofen el ibuprofeno
ice el hielo; **~ hockey** el hockey sobre hielo
icy adj helado
identification el documento de identidad
ill v **(to feel)** encontrarse mal
in dentro
include v incluir
indoor pool la piscina cubierta
inexpensive barato
infected infectado
information (phone) el número de teléfono de información; **~ desk** el mostrador de información
insect el insecto; **~ bite** la picadura de

insecto; **~ repellent** el repelente de insectos
insert v introducir
insomnia el insomnio
instant message el mensaje instantáneo
insulin la insulina
insurance el seguro; **~ card** la tarjeta de seguro; **~ company** la compañía de seguros
interesting interesante
intermediate el nivel intermedio
international (airport area) internacional; **~ flight** el vuelo internacional; **~ student card** la tarjeta internacional de estudiante
internet el internet; **~ cafe** el cibercafé; **~ service** el servicio de internet; **wireless ~** el acceso inalámbrico
interpreter el/la intérprete
intersection el cruce
intestine el intestino
introduce v presentar
invoice [BE] la factura
Ireland Irlanda
Irish irlandés
iron v planchar; **~** n **(clothes)** la plancha
Italian italiano

J

jacket la chaqueta
jar el bote

jaw la mandíbula
jazz el jazz; **~ club** el club de jazz
jeans los vaqueros
jet ski la moto acuática
jeweler la joyería
jewelry las joyas
join v acompañar a
joint (body part) la articulación

K

key la llave; **~ card** la llave electrónica; **~ ring** el llavero
kiddie pool la piscina infantil
kidney (body part) el riñón
kilo el kilo; **~gram** el kilogramo; **~meter** el kilómetro
kiss v besar
kitchen la cocina; **~ foil [BE]** el papel de aluminio
knee la rodilla
knife el cuchillo

L

lace el encaje
lactose intolerant alérgico a la lactosa
lake el lago
large grande; **~er** más grande
last último
late (time) tarde; **~er** más tarde
launderette [BE] la lavandería
laundromat la lavandería

laundry la colada; ~
  facility la lavan-
  dería; ~ **service** el
  servicio de lavandería
lawyer el abogado
leather el cuero
to leave v salir
left (direction) la
  izquierda
leg la pierna
lens la lente
less menos
lesson la lección
letter la carta
library la biblioteca
life la vida; ~
  jacket el
  chaleco salvavidas;
  ~guard el socorrista
lift n **[BE]** el ascensor;
  ~ v **(to give a
  ride)** llevar en
  coche; ~ **pass**
  el pase de acceso a
  los remontes
light (overhead) la
  luz; ~ v **(ciga-
  rette)** dar fuego;
  ~bulb la bombilla
lighter el mechero
like v gustar; **I like**
  me gusta
line (train) la línea
linen el lino
lip el labio
liquor store la
  tienda de bebidas
  alcohólicas
liter el litro
little pequeño
live v vivir
liver (body part) el
  hígado
loafers los mocasines

local de la zona
lock v cerrar; ~ n el
  cerrojo
locker la taquilla
**log on (com-
  puter)** iniciar sesión
log off v **(com-
  puter)** cerrar sesión
long largo; ~ **sleeves**
  las mangas largas;
  ~-sighted [BE]
  hipermétrope
look v mirar
lose v **(some-
  thing)** perder
lost perdido; ~ **and
  found** la oficina de
  objetos perdidos
lotion la crema
  hidratante
louder más alto
love v querer; ~ n
  el amor
low bajo; **~er** más
  bajo
luggage el equipaje;
  ~ **cart** el carrito de
  equipaje; ~ **locker**
  la consigna automáti-
  ca; ~ **ticket** el talón
  de equipaje; **hand
  ~ [BE]** el equipaje
  de mano
lunch la comida
lung el pulmón

M

magazine la revista
magnificent magnífico
mail v enviar por
  correo; ~ n el correo;
  ~box el buzón
  de correo
main principal; ~

attractions
  los principales
  sitios de interés;
  ~ **course** el plato
  principal
**make up a
  prescription** v
  [BE] despachar
  medicamentos
mall el centro
  comercial
man el hombre
manager el gerente
manicure la manicura
manual car el coche
  con transmisión
  manual
map el mapa
market el mercado
married casado
marry v casarse
**mass (church
  service)** la misa
massage el masaje
match la cerilla
meal la comida
measure v **(some-
  one)** medir
measuring cup la taza
  medidora
measuring spoon la
  cuchara medidora
mechanic el mecánico
medicine el medica-
  mento
medium (size) me-
  diano
meet v **(some-
  one)** conocer
meeting la reunión;
  ~ **room** la sala de
  reuniones
membership card la
  tarjeta de socio

memorial (place) el
  monumento
  conmemorativo
memory card la
  tarjeta de memoria
mend v zurcir
**menstrual
  cramps** los dolores
  menstruales
menu la carta
message el mensaje
meter (parking) el
  parquímetro
microwave el
  microondas
midday [BE] el
  mediodía
midnight la medi-
  anoche
mileage el kilometraje
mini-bar el minibar
minute el minuto
missing desaparecido
mistake el error
mobile móvil; ~
  home la caravana;
  ~ **phone [BE]**
  el teléfono móvil
mobility la movilidad
money el dinero
month el mes
mop la fregona
moped el ciclomotor
more más
morning la mañana
mosque la mezquita
mother la madre
motion sickness el
  mareo
motor el motor; ~
  boat la lancha
  motora; **~cycle** la
  motocicleta; **~way
  [BE]** la autopista

mountain la montaña;
~ bike la bicicleta
de montaña
mousse (hair) la
espuma para el pelo
mouth *n* la boca
movie la película; **~
theater** el cine
mug *v* asaltar
muscle (body part) el
músculo
museum el museo
music la música; **~
store** la tienda de
música

N

nail la uña; **~ file** la
lima de uñas; **~
salon** el salon de
manicura
name el nombre
napkin la servilleta
nappy [BE] el pañale
nationality la
nacionalidad
nature preserve la
reserva natural
(be) nauseous *v* tener
náuseas
near cerca;
~-sighted miope;
~by cerca de aquí
neck el cuello
necklace el collar
need *v* necesitar
newspaper el
periódico
newsstand el quiosco
next próximo
nice *adj* amable
night la noche; **~club**
la discoteca
no no

non sin; **~-alco-
holic** sin alcohol;
~-smoking para no
fumadores
noon el mediodía
north el norte
nose la nariz
note [BE] el billete
nothing nada
notify *v* avisar
**novice (skill
level)** principiante
now ahora
number el número
nurse el enfermero/la
enfermera

O

office la oficina; **~
hours (doctor's)** las
horas de consulta;
**~ hours (other of-
fices)** el horario de
oficina
off-licence [BE] la
tienda de bebidas
alcohólicas
oil el aceite
OK de acuerdo
old *adj* viejo
on the corner en la
esquina
once una vez
one uno; **~-way
ticket** el billete
de ida; **~-way
street** la calle de
sentido único
only solamente
open *v* abrir; **~** *adj*
abierto
opera la ópera; **~
house** el teatro de
la ópera

opposite frente a
optician el oculista
orange (color) naranja
orchestra la orquesta
order *v* pedir
outdoor pool la
piscina exterior
outside fuera
over sobre; **~
the counter
(medication)** sin
receta; **~look
(scenic place)** el
mirador; **~night** por
la noche
oxygen treatment
la oxigenoterapia

P

p.m. de la tarde
pacifier el chupete
pack *v* hacer las
maletas
package el paquete
paddling pool [BE] la
piscina infantil
pad [BE] la compresa
pain el dolor
pajamas los pijamas
palace el palacio
pants los pantalones
pantyhose las medias
paper el papel; **~
towel** el papel de
cocina
paracetamol [BE] el
paracetamol
park *v* aparcar;
~ *n* el parque;
~ing garage el
párking; **~ing lot** el
aparcamiento
**parliament build-
ing** el palacio de las

cortes
part (for car) la pieza;
~-time a tiempo
parcial
pass through *v* estar
de paso
passenger el pasajero
passport el pasaporte;
~ control el control
de pasaportes
password la
contraseña
pastry shop la
pastelería
path el camino
pay *v* pagar; **~
phone** el teléfono
público
**peak (of a moun-
tain)** la cima
pearl la perla
pedestrian el peatón
pediatrician el
pediatra
pedicure la pedicura
pen el bolígrafo
penicillin la penicilina
penis el pene
per por; **~ day** por
día; **~ hour** por
hora; **~ night** por
noche; **~ week** por
semana
perfume el perfume
period (menstrual) la
regla; **~ (of time)** la
época
permit *v* permitir
petite las tallas
pequeñas
petrol la gasolina; **~
station** la gaso-
linera
pewter el peltre

pharmacy la farmacia
phone v
  hacer una llamada;
  ~ n el teléfono; ~
  call la llamada de
  teléfono; ~ **card** la
  tarjeta telefónica; ~
  number el número
  de teléfono
photo la foto;
  ~copy la fotocopia;
  ~graphy la foto-
  grafía
pick up v **(some-**
  thing) recoger
picnic area la zona
  para picnic
piece el trozo
Pill (birth control) la
  píldora
pillow la almohada
personal identifica-
  tion number
  (PIN) la clave
pink rosa
piste [BE] la pista; ~
  map [BE] el mapa
  de pistas
pizzeria la pizzería
place v **(a bet)** hacer
  una apuesta
plane el avión
plastic wrap el film
  transparente
plate el plato
platform [BE]
  (train) el andén
platinum el platino
play v jugar; ~ n
  (theater) la obra de
  teatro; **~ground** el
  patio de recreo;
  ~pen el parque
please por favor

pleasure el placer
plunger el desa-
  tascador
plus size la talla
  grande
pocket el bolsillo
poison el veneno
poles (skiing) los
  bastones
police la policía; ~
  report el certificado
  de la policía; ~ **sta-**
  tion la comisaría
pond el estanque
pool la piscina
pop music la música
  pop
portion la ración
post [BE] el correo;
  ~ **office** la oficina
  de correos; **~box**
  [BE] el buzón de
  correos; **~card** la
  tarjeta postal
pot la olla
pottery la cerámica
pounds (British
  sterling) las libras
  esterlinas
pregnant embarazada
prescribe v recetar
prescription la receta
press v **(cloth-**
  ing) planchar
price el precio
print v imprimir
problem el problema
produce las frutas y
  verduras; ~ **store** la
  frutería y verdulería
prohibit v prohibir
pronounce v
  pronunciar
public el público

pull v **(door sign)** tirar
purple morado
purse el bolso
push v **(door**
  sign) empujar;
  ~chair [BE] el
  cochecito de niño

Q

quality n la calidad
question la pregunta
quiet adj tranquilo

R

racetrack el circuito
  de carreras
racket (sports) la
  raqueta
railway station
  [BE] la estación de
  trenes
rain la lluvia;
  ~coat el chubas-
  quero; **~forest** el
  bosque pluvial;
  ~y adv lluvioso
rap (music) el rap
rape v violar; ~ n la
  violación
rash la erupción
  cutánea
razor blade la hoja de
  afeitar
reach v localizar
ready listo
real auténtico
receipt el recibo
receive v recibir
reception la recepción
recharge v recargar
recommend v
  recomendar
recommendation la
  recomendación

recycle v reciclar
red rojo
refrigerator n la
  nevera
region la región
registered mail el
  correo certificado
regular normal
relationship la
  relación
rent v alquilar
rental car el coche de
  alquiler
repair v arreglar
repeat v repetir
reservation la
  reserva;
  ~ **desk** la taquilla
reserve v reservar
restaurant el
  restaurante
restroom el servicio
retired jubilado
return v **(some-**
  thing) devolver; ~ n
  [BE] la ida y vuelta
rib (body part) la
  costilla
right (direction) derecha; ~ **of way** prioridad de paso
ring el anillo
river n el río
road map el mapa de
  carreteras
rob v atracar
robbed atracado
romantic romántico
room la habitación;
  ~ **key** la llave de
  habitación; ~ **ser-**
  vice el servicio de
  habitaciones
round-trip ida y vuelta

route la ruta
rowboat la barca de remos
rubbish [BE] la basura; **~ bag [BE]** la bolsa de basura
rugby el rugby
ruins las ruinas
rush la prisa

S

sad triste
safe *n* la caja fuerte; ~ *adj* seguro
sales tax el IVA
same mismo
sandals las sandalias
sanitary napkin la compresa
saucepan el cazo
sauna la sauna
save *v* (**computer**) guardar
savings (account) la cuenta de ahorro
scanner el escáner
scarf la bufanda
schedule *v* programar; ~ *n* el horario
school el colegio
science la ciencia
scissors las tijeras
sea el mar
seat el asiento
security la seguridad
see *v* ver
self-service el autoservicio
sell *v* vender
seminar el seminario
send *v* enviar
senior citizen jubilado
separated (marriage) -separado

serious serio
service (in a restaurant) el servicio
sexually transmitted disease (STD) la enfermedad de transmisión sexual
shampoo el champú
sharp afilado
shaving cream la crema de afeitar
sheet la sábana
ship *v* enviar
shirt la camisa
shoe store la zapatería
shoes los zapatos
shop *v* comprar
shopping ir de compras; **~ area** la zona de compras; **~ centre [BE]** el centro comercial; **~ mall** el centro comercial
short corto; **~ sleeves** las mangas cortas; **~s** los pantalones cortos; **~-sighted [BE]** miope
shoulder el hombro
show *v* enseñar
shower la ducha
shrine el santuario
sick enfermo
side el lado; **~ dish** la guarnición; **~ effect** el efecto secundario; **~ order** la guarnición
sightsee *v* hacer turismo
sightseeing tour el recorrido turístico

sign *v* (**name**) firmar
silk la seda
silver la plata
single (unmarried) soltero; **~ bed** la cama; **~ prints** una copia; **~ room** una habitación individual
sink el lavabo
sister la hermana
sit *v* sentarse
size la talla
skin la piel
skirt la falda
ski *v* esquiar; ~ *n* el esquí; **~ lift** el telesquí
sleep *v* dormir; **~er car** el coche cama; **~ing bag** el saco de dormir
slice *v* cortar en rodajas
slippers las zapatillas
slower más despacio
slowly despacio
small pequeño
smaller más pequeño
smoke *v* fumar
smoking (area) la zona de fumadores
snack bar la cafetería
sneakers las zapatillas de deporte
snorkeling equipment el equipo de esnórquel
snow la nieve; **~board** la tabla de snowboard; **~shoe** la raqueta de nieve; **~y** nevado
soap el jabón

soccer el fútbol
sock el calcetín
some alguno
soother [BE] el chupete
sore throat las anginas
sorry lo siento
south el sur
souvenir el recuerdo; **~ store** la tienda de recuerdos
spa el centro de salud y belleza
Spain España
Spanish el español
spatula la espátula
speak *v* hablar
special (food) la especialidad de la casa
specialist (doctor) el especialista
specimen el ejemplar
speeding el exceso de velocidad
spell *v* deletrear
spicy picante
spine (body part) la columna vertebral
spoon la cuchara
sports los deportes; **~ massage** el masaje deportivo
sporting goods store la tienda de deportes
sprain el esguince
square cuadrado; **~ kilometer** el kilómetro cuadrado; **~ meter** el metro cuadrado
stadium el estadio

stairs las escaleras

stamp v (**a ticket**) picar; ~ n (**postage**) el sello

start v empezar

starter [BE] el aperitivo

station la estación; **bus** ~ la estación de autobuses; **gas** ~ la gasolinera; **muster** ~ [BE] el punto de reunión; **petrol** ~ [BE] la gasolinera; **subway** ~ el metro; **train** ~ la estación de tren

statue la estatua

stay v quedarse

steal v robar

steep empinado

sterling silver la plata esterlina

sting el escozor

stolen robado

stomach el estómago; ~**ache** el dolor de estómago

stop v pararse; ~ n la parada

storey [BE] la planta

stove el horno

straight recto

strange extraño

stream el arroyo

stroller el cochecito

student el estudiante

study v estudiar

stunning impresionante

subtitle el subtítulo

subway el metro; ~ **station** la estación

de metro

suit el traje

suitcase la maleta

sun el sol; ~**block** el protector solar total; ~**burn** la quemadura solar; ~**glasses** las gafas de sol; ~**ny** soleado; ~**screen** el protector solar; ~**stroke** la insolación

super (fuel) súper; ~**market** el supermercado

surfboard la tabla de surf

surgical spirit [BE] el alcohol etílico

swallow v tragar

sweater el jersey

sweatshirt la sudadera

sweet (taste) dulce; ~**s** [BE] los caramelos

swelling la hinchazón

swim v nadar; ~**suit** el bañador

symbol (keyboard) el símbolo

synagogue la sinagoga

T

table la mesa

tablet (medicine) el comprimido

take v llevar; ~ **away** [BE] para llevar

tampon el tampón

tapas bar el bar de tapas

taste v probar

taxi el taxi

team el equipo

telephone el teléfono

temporary provisional

tennis el tenis

tent la tienda de campaña; ~ **peg** la estaca; ~ **pole** el mástil

terminal (airport) la terminal

terracotta la terracotta

terrible terrible

text v (**send a message**) enviar un mensaje de texto; ~ n (**message**) el texto

thank v dar las gracias a; ~ **you** gracias

that eso

theater el teatro

there ahí

thief el ladrón

thigh el muslo

thirsty sediento

this esto

throat la garganta

ticket el billete; ~ **office** el despacho de billetes; ~**ed passenger** el pasajero con billete

tie (clothing) la corbata

time el tiempo; ~**table** [BE] el horario

tire la rueda

tired cansado

tissue el pañuelo de paper

tobacconist el estanco

today hoy

toe el dedo del pie; ~**nail** la uña del pie

toilet [BE] el servicio; ~ **paper** el papel higiénico

tomorrow mañana

tongue la lengua

tonight esta noche

too demasiado

tooth el diente; ~**brush** el cepillo de dientes; ~**paste** la pasta de dientes

total (amount) el total

tough (food) duro

tourist el turista; ~ **information office** la oficina de turismo

tour el recorrido turístico

tow truck la grúa

towel la toalla

tower la torre

town la ciudad; ~ **hall** el ayuntamiento; ~ **map** el mapa de ciudad; ~ **square** la plaza

toy el juguete; ~ **store** la tienda de juguetes

track (train) el andén

traditional tradicional

traffic light el semáforo

trail la pista; ~ **map** el mapa de la pista

trailer el remolque

train el tren; ~ **station** la estación de tren

transfer v cambiar
translate v traducir
trash la basura
travel v viajar; ~ **agency** la agencia de viajes; ~ **sickness** el mareo; **~er's check [cheque BE]** el cheque de viaje
tree el árbol
trim (hair cut) cortarse las puntas
trip el viaje
trolley [BE] el carrito
trousers [BE] los pantalones
T-shirt la camiseta
turn off v apagar
turn on v encender
TV la televisión
type v escribir a máquina
tyre [BE] la rueda

U

United Kingdom (U.K.) el Reino Unido
United States (U.S.) los Estados Unidos
ugly feo
umbrella el paraguas
unattended desatendido
unconscious inconsciente
underground [BE] el metro; ~ **station [BE]** la estación de metro
underpants [BE] los calzoncillos

understand v entender
underwear la ropa interior
university la universidad
unleaded (gas) la gasolina sin plomo
upper superior
urgent urgente
use v usar
username el nombre de usuario
utensil el cubierto

V

vacancy la habitación libre
vacation las vacaciones
vaccination la vacuna
vacuum cleaner la aspiradora
vaginal infection la infección vaginal
valid validez
valley el valle
valuable valioso
VAT [BE] el IVA
vegetarian vegetariano
vehicle registration el registro del coche
viewpoint [BE] el mirador
village el pueblo
vineyard la viña
visa (passport document) el visado
visit v visitar; **~ing hours** el horario de visita
visually impaired la persona con

discapacidad visual
vitamin la vitamina
V-neck el cuello de pico
vomit v vomitar

W

wait v esperar; ~ n la espera; **~ing room** la sala de espera
waiter el camarero
waitress la camarera
wake v despertarse; **~-up call** la llamada despertador
walk v caminar; ~ n la caminata; **~ing route** la ruta de senderismo
wallet la cartera
warm v (something) calentar; ~ adj (temperature) calor
washing machine la lavadora
watch el reloj
waterfall la cascada
weather el tiempo
week la semana; **~end** el fin de semana; **~ly** semanal
welcome v acoger
well bien; **~-rested** descansado
west el oeste
what (question) qué
wheelchair la silla de ruedas; **~ ramp** la rampa para silla de ruedas
when (question) cuándo

where (question) dónde
white blanco; ~ **gold** el oro blanco
who (question) quién
widowed viudo
wife la mujer
window la ventana; **~ case** el escaparate
windsurfer el surfista
wine list la carta de vinos
wireless inalámbrico; ~ **internet** el acceso inalámbrico a internet; ~ **internet service** el servicio inalámbrico a internet; ~ **phone** el teléfono móvil
with con
withdraw v retirar; **~al (bank)** retirar fondos
without sin
woman la mujer
wool la lana
work v trabajar
wrap v envolver
wrist la muñeca
write v escribir

Y

year el año
yellow amarillo
yes sí
yesterday ayer
young joven
youth hostel el albergue juvenil

Z

zoo el zoológico

SPANISH–ENGLISH

A

a tiempo completo full-time

a tiempo parcial part-time

la abadía abbey

el abanico fan (souvenir)

abierto *adj* open

el abogado lawyer

abrazar *v* hug

el abrebotellas bottle opener

el abrelatas can opener

el abrigo coat

abrir *v* open

el abuelo grandparent

aburrido boring

acampar *v* camp

el acantilado cliff

el acceso access; **~ inalámbrico a internet** wireless internet; **~ para discapacitados** handicapped- [disabled-BE] accessible

el accidente accident

el aceite oil

aceptar *v* accept

acoger *v* welcome

acompañar a *v* join

la acupuntura acupuncture

el adaptador adapter

adicional extra

adiós goodbye

las aduanas customs

el aeropuerto airport

afilado sharp

la agencia agency; **~ de viajes** travel agency

agotado exhausted

el agua water; **~ caliente** hot water; **~ potable** drinking water

las aguas termales hot spring

ahí there

ahora now

el aire air, air pump; **~ acondicionado** air conditioning

el albergue hostel; **~ juvenil** youth hostel

alérgico allergic; **~ a la lactosa** lactose intolerant

algo anything

el algodón cotton

alguno some

alimentar *v* feed

el allanamiento de morada break-in (burglary)

la almohada pillow

el alojamiento accommodation

alquilar *v* rent [hire BE]; **el ~ de coches** car rental [hire BE]

alto high

amable nice

amarillo yellow

la ambulancia ambulance

el amigo friend

el amor *n* love

el andén track [platform BE] (train)

anémico anemic

la anestesia anesthesia

las anginas sore throat

el anillo ring

el animal animal

antes de before

el antibiótico antibiotic

el año year

apagar *v* turn off

el aparcamiento parking lot [car park BE]

aparcar *v* park

el apartamento apartment

el apéndice appendix (body part)

el aperitivo appetizer [starter BE]

aquí here

el árbol tree

la aromaterapia aromatherapy

arreglar *v* repair

el arroyo stream

la arteria artery

la articulación joint (body part)

los artículos goods; **~ para el hogar** household good

la artritis arthritis

asaltar *v* mug

el asalto attack

el ascensor elevator [lift BE]

asiático Asian

el asiento seat; **~ de niño** car seat; **~ de pasillo** aisle seat

asistir *v* attend

asmático asthmatic

la aspiradora vacuum cleaner

la aspirina aspirin

atracado robbed

atracar *v* rob

Australia Australia

australiano Australian

auténtico real

el autobús bus; **~ rápido** express bus

automático automatic

la autopista highway [motorway BE]

el autoservicio self-service

la avería breakdown

el avión airplane, plane

avisar *v* notify

ayer yesterday

la ayuda *n* help

ayudar *v* help

el ayuntamiento town hall

azul blue

B

bailar *v* dance

bajarse *v* get off (a train, bus, subway)

bajo low
el ballet ballet
el baloncesto basketball
el bálsamo para después del afeitado aftershave
el banco bank
el bañador swimsuit
el baño bathroom
el bar bar; ~ **de tapas** tapas bar; ~ **gay** gay bar
barato cheap, inexpensive
la barbacoa barbecue
la barca de remos rowboat
el barco boat
los bastones poles (skiing)
la basura trash [rubbish BE]
la batería battery (car)
el bebé baby
beber v drink
la bebida n drink
beis beige
el béisbol baseball
besar v kiss
el biberón baby bottle
la biblioteca library
la bicicleta bicycle; ~ **de montaña** mountain bike
el billete n bill (money); ~ ticket; ~ **de autobús** bus ticket; ~ **de ida** one-way (ticket); ~ **de ida y vuelta** round trip [return BE]; ~ **electrónico** e-ticket

el biquini bikini
blanco white
la blusa blouse
la boca mouth
el bolígrafo pen
la bolsa de basura garbage [rubbish BE] bag
el bolsillo pocket
el bolso purse [handbag BE]
los bomberos fire department
la bombilla lightbulb
borrar v clear (on an ATM); ~ v delete (computer)
el bosque forest; ~ **pluvial** rainforest
las botas boots; ~ **de montaña** hiking boots
el bote jar
la botella bottle
el brazo arm
británico British
el broche brooch
bucear to dive
bueno adj good
buenas noches good evening
buenas tardes good afternoon
buenos días good morning
la bufanda scarf
el buzón de correo mailbox [postbox BE]

C

la cabaña cabin (house)
el cabaré cabaret

la cabeza head (body part)
la cafetería cafe, coffee shop, snack bar
la caja case (amount); ~ **fuerte** n safe
el cajero cashier; ~ **automático** ATM
el calcetín sock
la calefacción heater [heating BE]
calentar v heat, warm
la calidad quality
la calle de sentido único one-way street
calor hot, warm (temperature)
las calorías calories
los calzoncillos briefs [underpants BE] (clothing)
la cama single bed; ~ **de matrimonio** double bed
la cámara camera; ~ **digital** digital camera
la camarera waitress
el camarero waiter
el camarote cabin (ship)
cambiar v change, exchange, transfer
el cambio n change (money); ~ **de divisas** currency exchange
caminar v walk
la caminata n walk
el camino path
la camisa shirt
la camiseta T-shirt
el cámping campsite

el campo field (sports); ~ **de batalla** battleground; ~ **de golf** golf course
Canadá Canada
canadiense Canadian
cancelar v cancel
el/la canguro babysitter
cansado tired
el cañón canyon
la cara face
los caramelos candy [sweets BE]
la caravana mobile home
el carbón charcoal
el carnicero butcher
caro expensive
el carrete film (camera)
el carrito cart [trolley BE] (grocery store); ~ **de equipaje** luggage cart
la carta letter
la carta n menu; ~ **de bebidas** drink menu; ~ **para niños** children's menu; ~ **de vinos** wine list
la cartera n wallet
el cartón carton; ~ **de tabaco** carton of cigarettes
la casa house; ~ **de cambio** currency exchange office
casado married
casarse v marry
la cascada waterfall
el casco helmet

los cascos headphones

el casino casino

el castillo castle

el catarro cold (sickness)

la catedral cathedral

el catre cot

causar daño v damage

el cazo saucepan

el CD CD

la cena dinner

el centímetro centimeter

el centro downtown area; ~ **comercial** shopping mall [centre BE]; ~ **de negocios** business center; ~ **de salud y belleza** spa

el cepillo de pelo hair brush

la cerámica pottery

cerca near; ~ **de aquí** nearby

la cerilla v match

cerrado closed

cerrar v close, lock; ~ **sesión** v log off (computer)

el cerrojo n lock

el certificado certificate; ~ **de la policía** police report

la cesta basket (grocery store)

el chaleco salvavidas life jacket

el champú shampoo

la chaqueta jacket

la charcutería delicatessen

el cheque n check [cheque BE] (payment); ~ **de viaje** traveler's check [cheque BE]

el chicle chewing gum

chino Chinese

el chubasquero raincoat

el chupete pacifier [soother BE]

el cibercafé internet cafe

el ciclismo cycling

el ciclomotor moped

la ciencia science

el cigarrillo cigarette

la cima peak (of a mountain)

el cine movie theater

la cinta transportadora conveyor belt

el cinturón n belt

el circuito de carreras racetrack

la cita appointment

la ciudad town

la clase class; ~ **económica** economy class; ~ **preferente** business class

la clave personal identification number (PIN)

el club de jazz jazz club

cobrar v bill (charge); ~ v cash; ~ v charge (credit card)

el cobre copper

el coche n car; ~ **de alquiler** rental (hire BE] car; ~ **automáti-**

co automatic car; ~ **cama** sleeper [sleeping BE] car; ~ **con transmisión manual** manual car

el cochecito stroller [pushchair BE]

la cocina kitchen

cocinar v cook

el código de país country code

el codo elbow

la colada laundry

el colegio school

la colina hill

el collar necklace

la colonia cologne

el color color

la columna vertebral spine (body part)

el comedor dining room

comer v eat

la comida food, lunch, meal; ~ **rápida** fast food

la comisaría police station

cómo how

el compañero de trabajo colleague

la compañia company; ~ **aérea** airline; ~ **de seguros** insurance company

comprar v buy, shop

la compresa sanitary napkin [pad BE]

el comprimido tablet (medicine)

con with; ~ **plomo** leaded (gas)

el concierto concert

conducir v drive

conectarse v connect (internet)

la conexión connection (internet); ~ **de vuelo** connection (flight)

la conferencia conference

confirmar v confirm

el congelador freezer

la congestión congestion

conocer v meet (someone)

la consigna automática luggage locker

el consulado Consulate

el consultor consultant

contagioso contagious

la contraseña password

el control de pasaportes passport control

el corazón heart

la corbata tie (clothing)

el correo n mail [post BE]; ~ **aéreo** airmail; ~ **certificado** registered mail; ~ **electrónico** n e-mail

cortar v cut (hair); ~ **en rodajas** to slice

cortarse las puntas v trim (hair cut)

el corte n cut (injury); ~ **de pelo** haircut

corto short

costar v cost

la costilla rib (body part)

la crema cream; **~ antiséptica** antiseptic cream; **~ de afeitar** shaving cream; **~ hidratante** lotion

el cristal crystal

el cruce intersection

cuándo when (question)

cuánto cuesta how much

el cubierto utensil

la cuchara spoon; **~ medidora** measuring spoon

la cucharadita teaspoon

la cuchilla desechable disposable razor

el cuchillo knife

el cuello neck; **~ de pico** V-neck; **~ redondo** crew neck

el cuenco bowl

la cuenta account; **~ de ahorro** savings account; **~ corriente** checking account (current BE) account

cuero leather

la cueva cave

el cumpleaños birthday

la cuna crib

D

dar to give; **~ el pecho** breastfeed; **~ fuego** light (cigarette); **~ las gracias a** v thank

de from, of; **~ acuerdo** OK; **~ la mañana** a.m.; **~ la tarde** p.m.; **~ la zona** local

declarar v declare

el dedo finger; **~ del pie** toe

deletrear v spell

delicioso delicious

la dentadura denture

el dentista dentist

dentro in

la depilacion wax; **~ de cejas** eyebrow wax; **~ de las ingles** bikini wax

deportes sports

depositar v deposit

el depósito bancario deposit (bank)

la derecha right (direction)

desaparecido missing

el desatascador plunger

desatendido unattended

el desayuno breakfast

descansado well-rested

desconectar v disconnect (computer)

el descuento discount

desechable disposable

el desierto desert

el desodorante deodorant

despachar medicamentos v fill (make up BE) a prescription

el despacho de billetes ticket office

despacio slowly

despertarse v wake

después after

el detergente detergent

detrás de behind (direction)

devolver v exchange, return (goods)

el día day

diabético diabetic

el diamante diamond

la diarrea diarrhea

el diente tooth

el diesel diesel

difícil difficult

digital digital

el dinero money

la dirección direction

la dirección address; **~ de correo electrónico** e-mail address

discapacitado handicapped (disabled BE)

la discoteca club (dance, night); **~ gay** gay club

disculparse v excuse (to get attention)

disfrutar v enjoy

disponible available

divorciar v divorce

doblada dubbed

doblando (la esquina) around (the corner)

la docena dozen

el documento de identidad identification

el dólar dollar (U.S.)

el dolor pain; **~ de cabeza** headache; **~ de espalda** backache; **~ de estómago** stomachache; **~ de oído** earache; **~ de pecho** chest pain

los dolores menstruales menstrual cramps

dónde where (question)

dormir v sleep

el dormitorio dormitory

la ducha shower

dulce sweet (taste)

durante during

el DVD DVD

E

la edad age

el edificio building

el efectivo cash

el efecto secundario side effect

el ejemplar specimen

embarazada pregnant

embarcar v board

la emergencia emergency

el empaste filling (tooth)

empezar v begin, start

empinado steep

empujar v push (door sign)

en la esquina on the corner

el encaje lace

encender v turn on

el enchufe eléctrico electric outlet

encontrarse mal *v* be ill

la enfermedad de transmisión sexual sexually transmitted disease (STD)

el enfermero/la enfermera nurse

enfermo sick

enseñar *v* show

entender *v* understand

la entrada admission/ cover charge; ~ entrance

entrar *v* enter

el entretenimiento entertainment

enviar *v* send, ship; ~ **por correo** *v* mail; ~ **un correo electrónico** *v* e-mail; ~ **un fax** *v* fax; ~ **un mensaje de texto** *v* text (send a message)

envolver *v* wrap

la época period (of time)

el equipaje luggage [baggage BE]; ~ **de mano** carry-on (piece of hand luggage)

el equipo team

el equipo equipment; ~ **de buceo** diving equipment; ~ **de esnórquel** snorkeling equipment

equis ele (XL) extra large

el error mistake

la erupción cutánea rash

las escaleras stairs; ~ **mecánicas** escalators

el escáner scanner

el escaparate window case

la escoba broom

el escozor sting

escribir *v* write; ~ **a máquina** *v* type

el escurridor colander

el esguince sprain

el esmalte enamel (jewelry)

eso that

la espalda back

España Spain

el español Spanish

la espátula spatula

la especialidad de la casa special (food)

el especialista specialist (doctor)

la espera *n* wait

esperar *v* wait

la espuma para el pelo mousse (hair)

el esquí *n* ski

esquiar *v* ski

los esquís acuáticos water skis

esta noche tonight

la estaca tent peg

la estación station; ~ **de autobuses** bus station; ~ **de metro** subway [underground BE] station; ~ **de tren** train [railway BE] station

el estadio stadium

el estado de salud condition (medical)

los Estados Unidos United States (U.S.)

estadounidense American

el estanco tobacconist

el estanque pond

estar *v* be; ~ **de paso** *v* pass through

la estatua statue

el este east

el estilista hairstylist

esto this

el estómago stomach

estrellarse *v* crash (car)

estreñido constipated

estudiando studying

el estudiante student

estudiar *v* study

el euro euro

el exceso excess; ~ **de velocidad** speeding

la excursión excursion

experto expert (skill level)

la extensión extension (phone)

extraer *v* extract (tooth)

extraño strange

F

fácil *adj* easy

la factura bill (invoice BE)

la facturación check-in (airport)

facturar check (luggage)

la falda skirt

la familia family

la farmacia pharmacy [chemist BE]

el fax *n* fax

la fecha date (calendar)

feliz *adj* happy

feo *adj* ugly

el ferry ferry

la fianza deposit (to reserve a room)

la fiebre fever

el film transparente plastic wrap (cling film BE]

el fin de semana weekend

firmar *v* sign (name)

la flor flower

la fórmula infantil formula (baby)

el formulario form

la foto exposure (film); ~ **photo**; ~**copia** photocopy; ~**grafía** photography; ~ **digital** digital photo

la fregona mop

los frenos brakes (car)

frente a opposite

fresco fresh

frío *adj* cold (temperature)

las frutas y verduras produce

la frutería y verdulería produce store

el fuego fire

la fuente fountain

fuera outside

el fuerte fort

fumar *v* smoke

la funda para la cámara camera case
el fútbol soccer [football BE]

G
las gafas glasses; **~ de sol** sunglasses
el garaje garage (parking)
la garganta throat
la garrafa carafe
el gas butano cooking gas
la gasolina gas [petrol BE]; **~ sin plomo** unleaded gas
la gasolinera gas [petrol BE] station
gay gay
el gerente manager
el gimnasio gym
el ginecólogo gynecologist
la gomina gel (hair)
la gota drop (medicine)
grabar *v* burn (CD); **~** *v* engrave
gracias thank you
los grados degrees (temperature); **~ centígrado** Celsius
el gramo gram
grande large
los grandes almacenes department store
la granja farm
gratuito free
gris gray
la grúa tow truck
el grupo group
guapo attractive

guardar *v* save (computer)
la guarnición side dish, order
el guía guide
la guía guide book; **~ de tiendas** store directory
gustar *v* like; **me gusta** I like

H
ha sufrido daños damaged
la habitación room; **~ individual** single room; **~ libre** vacancy
hablar *v* speak
hacer *v* have; **~ una apuesta** *v* place (a bet); **~ un arreglo** *v* alter; **~ una llamada** *v* phone; **~ las maletas** *v* pack; **~ turismo** sightseeing
hambriento hungry
helado icy
la hermana sister
el hermano brother
el hielo ice
el hígado liver (body part)
la hinchazón swelling
hipermétrope far-sighted [long-sighted BE]
el hipódromo horsetrack
el hockey hockey; **~ sobre hielo** ice hockey
la hoja de afeitar ra-

zor blade
hola hello
el hombre man
el hombro shoulder
hondo deeply
la hora hour
el horario *n* schedule [timetable BE]
los horarios hours; **~ de atención al público** business hours; **~ de oficina** office hours; **~ de visita** visiting hours
las horas de consulta office hours (doctor's)
el hornillo camp stove
el horno stove
el hospital hospital
el hotel hotel
hoy today
el hueso bone

I
el ibuprofeno ibuprofen
la ida y vuelta round-trip [return BE]
la iglesia church
impresionante stunning
imprimir *v* print
el impuesto duty (tax)
incluir *v* include
inconsciente unconscious
increíble amazing
la infección vaginal vaginal infection
infectado infected
el inglés English

iniciar sesión *v* log on (computer)
el insecto bug
la insolación sunstroke
el insomnio insomnia
la insulina insulin
interesante interesting
internacional international (airport area)
la internet internet
el/la intérprete interpreter
el intestino intestine
introducir *v* insert
ir a *v* go (somewhere)
ir de compras *v* go shopping
Irlanda Ireland
irlandés Irish
el IVA sales tax [VAT BE]
la izquierda left (direction)

J
el jabón soap
el jardín botánico botanical garden
el jazz jazz
el jersey sweater
joven young
las joyas jewelry
la joyería jeweler
jubilado retired
jugar *v* play
el juguete toy

K
el kilo kilo; **~gramo** kilogram; **~metraje** mileage

el kilómetro kilometer; **~ cuadrado** square kilometer

L

el labio lip
la laca hairspray
el ladrón thief
el lago lake
la lana wool
la lancha motora motor boat
largo long
el lavabo sink
la lavadora washing machine
la lavandería laundromat [launderette BE]
lavar v wash
el lavavajillas dishwasher
la lección lesson
lejos far
la lengua tongue
la lente lens
las lentillas de contacto contact lens
las letras arts
las libras esterlinas pounds (British sterling)
libre de impuestos duty-free
la librería bookstore
el libro book
la lima de uñas nail file
limpiar v clean
la limpieza de cutis facial
limpio adj clean
la línea line (train)
el lino linen
la linterna flashlight

el líquido liquid; **~ de lentillas de contacto** lens solution; **~ lavavajillas** dishwashing liquid
listo ready
la litera berth
el litro liter
la llamada n call; **~ de teléfono** phone call; **~ despertador** wake-up call
llamar v call
la llave key; **~ de habitación** room key; **~ electrónica** key card
el llavero key ring
las llegadas arrivals (airport)
llegar v arrive
llenar v fill
llevar v take; **~ en coche** lift (to give a ride)
la lluvia rain
lluvioso rainy
lo siento sorry
localizar v reach
la luz light (overhead)

M

la madre mother
magnífico magnificent
el malestar estomacal upset stomach
la maleta bag, suitcase
la mandíbula jaw
las mangas cortas short sleeves
las mangas largas long sleeves
la manicura manicure
la mano hand
la manta blanket
mañana tomorrow; **la ~** morning
el mapa map; **~ de carreteras** road map; **~ de ciudad** town map; **~ de la pista** trail [piste BE] map
el mar sea
marcar v dial
mareado dizzy
el mareo motion [travel BE] sickness
el marido husband
marrón brown
el martillo hammer
más more; **~ alto** louder; **~ bajo** lower; **~ barato** cheaper; **~ despacio** slower; **~ grande** larger; **~ pequeño** smaller; **~ rápido** faster; **~ tarde** later; **~ temprano** earlier
el masaje massage; **~ deportivo** sports massage
el mástil tent pole
el mecánico mechanic
el mechero lighter
la media hora half hour
mediano medium (size)
la medianoche midnight
el medicamento medicine

el médico doctor
medio half; **~ kilo** half-kilo; **~día** noon [midday BE]
medir v measure (someone)
mejor best
menos less
el mensaje message; **~ instantáneo** instant message
el mercado market
el mes month
la mesa table
el metro subway [underground BE]
el metro cuadrado square meter
la mezquita mosque
el microondas microwave
el minibar mini-bar
el minuto minute
el mirador overlook [viewpoint BE] (scenic place)
mirar v look
la misa mass (church service)
mismo same
los mocasines loafers
la mochila backpack
molestar v bother
la moneda coin, currency
mono cute
la montaña n mountain
el monumento conmemorativo memorial (place)
morado purple

el mostrador de información information desk

mostrar v display

la moto acuática jet ski

la motocicleta motorcycle

movilidad mobility

la mujer wife, woman

la multa fine (fee for breaking law)

la muñeca doll; ~ wrist

el músculo muscle

el museo museum

la música music; ~ **clásica** classical music; ~ **folk** folk music; ~ **pop** pop music

el muslo thigh

N

nacional domestic

la nacionalidad nationality

nada nothing

nadar v swim

las nalgas buttocks

naranja orange (color)

la nariz nose

necesitar v need

los negocios business

negro black

nevado snowy

la nevera refrigerator

el nieto grandchild

la niña girl

el niño boy, child

el nivel intermedio intermediate

no no

la noche evening, night

el nombre name; ~ **de usuario** username

normal regular

las normas de vestuario dress code

el norte north

la novia girlfriend

el novio boyfriend

el número number; ~ **de fax** fax number; ~ **de permiso de conducir** driver's license number; ~ **de teléfono** phone number; ~ **de teléfono de información** information (phone)

O

la obra de teatro n play (theater)

el oculista optician

el oeste west

la oficina office; ~ **de correos** post office; ~ **de objetos perdidos** lost and found; ~ **de turismo** tourist information office

el ojo eye

la olla pot

la ópera opera

el ordenador computer

la oreja ear

la orina urine

el oro gold; ~ **amarillo** yellow gold; ~ **blanco** white gold

la orquesta orchestra

oscuro dark

el otro camino alternate route

la oxígenoterapia oxygen treatment

P

padecer del corazón heart condition

el padre father

pagar v pay

el pájaro bird

el palacio palace; ~ **de las cortes** parliament building

los palillos chinos chopsticks

la panadería bakery

los pantalones pants [trousers BE]; ~ **cortos** shorts

el pañal diaper [nappy BE]

el pañuelo de paper tissue

el papel paper; ~ **de aluminio** aluminum [kitchen BE] foil; ~ **de cocina** paper towel; ~ **higiénico** toilet paper

el paquete package

para for; ~ **llevar** to go (take away BE); ~ **no fumadores** non-smoking

el paracetamol acetaminophen [paracetamol BE]

la parada n stop; ~ **de autobús** bus stop

el paraguas umbrella

pararse v stop

el párking parking garage

el parque playpen; ~ park; ~ **de atracciones** amusement park

el partido game; ~ **de fútbol** soccer [football BE]; ~ **de voleibol** volleyball game

el pasajero passenger; ~ **con billete** ticketed passenger

el pasaporte passport

el pase de acceso a los remontes lift pass

el pasillo aisle

la pasta de dientes toothpaste

la pastelería pastry shop

el patio de recreo playground

el peatón pedestrian

el pecho chest (body part)

el pediatra pediatrician

la pedicura pedicure

pedir v order

el peinado hairstyle

el peine comb

la película movie

peligroso dangerous

el pelo hair

el peltre pewter

la peluquería de caballeros barber

la peluquería hair salon

los pendientes earrings
el pene penis
la penicilina penicillin
la pensión bed and breakfast
pequeño small
perder v lose (something)
perdido lost
el perfume perfume
el periódico newspaper
la perla pearl
permitir v allow, permit
el perro guía guide dog
la persona con discapacidad visual visually impaired person
la picadura de insecto insect bite
picante spicy
picar v stamp (a ticket)
el pie foot
la piel skin
la pierna leg
la pieza part (for car)
los pijamas pajamas
la pila battery
la píldora Pill (birth control)
la piscina pool; ~ **cubierta** indoor pool; ~ **exterior** outdoor pool; ~ **infantil** kiddie [paddling BE] pool
la pista trail [piste BE]
la pizzería pizzeria

el placer pleasure
la plancha n iron (clothes)
planchar v iron
la planta floor [storey BE]; ~ **baja** ground floor
la plata silver; ~ **esterlina** sterling silver
el platino platinum
el plato dish (kitchen); ~ **principal** main course
la playa beach
la plaza town square
la policía police
la pomada cream (ointment)
ponerse en contacto con v contact
por for; ~ per; ~ **día** per day; ~ **favor** please; ~ **hora** per hour; ~ **la noche** overnight; ~ **noche** per night; ~ **semana** per week
el postre dessert
el precio price
precioso beautiful
el prefijo area code
la pregunta question
presentar v introduce
el preservativo condom
la primera clase first class
primero first
los principales sitios de interés main attraction
principiante beginner, novice (skill level)

la prioridad de paso right of way
la prisa rush
el probador fitting room
probar v taste
el problema problem
el producto good; ~ **de limpieza** cleaning product
programar v schedule
prohibir v prohibit
el pronóstico forecast
pronunciar v pronounce
el protector solar sunscreen
provisional temporary
próximo next
el público public
el pueblo village
el puente bridge
la puerta gate (airport); ~ door; ~ **de incendios** fire door
el pulmón lung
la pulsera bracelet
el puro cigar

Q

qué what (question)
quedar bien v fit (clothing)
quedarse v stay
la queja complaint
la quemadura solar sunburn
querer v love (someone)
quién who (question)
el quiosco newsstand

R

la ración portion; ~ **para niños** children's portion
la rampa para silla de ruedas wheelchair ramp
el rap rap (music)
rápido express, fast
la raqueta racket (sports); ~ **de nieve** snowshoe
la reacción alérgica allergic reaction
recargar v recharge
la recepción reception
la receta prescription
recetar v prescribe
rechazar v decline (credit card)
recibir v receive
el recibo receipt
reciclar recycling
recoger v pick up (something)
la recogida de equipajes baggage claim
la recomendación recommendation
recomendar v recommend
el recorrido tour; ~ **en autobús** bus tour; ~ **turístico** sightseeing tour
recto straight
el recuerdo souvenir
el regalo gift
la región region
el registro check-in (hotel); ~ **del coche** vehicle registration

la regla period (menstrual)

el Reino Unido United Kingdom (U.K.)

la relación relationship

rellenar v fill out (form)

el reloj watch; ~ **de pared** wall clock

el remolque trailer

reparar v fix (repair)

el repelente de insectos insect repellent

repetir v repeat

la resaca hangover

la reserva reservation; ~ **natural** nature preserve

reservar v reserve

el/la residente de la UE EU resident

respirar v breathe

el restaurante restaurant

retirar v withdraw; ~ **fondos** withdrawal (bank)

retrasarse v delay

la reunión meeting

revelar v develop (film)

revisar v check (on something)

la revista magazine

el riñón kidney (body part)

el río river

robado stolen

robar v steal

el robo theft

la rodilla knee

rojo red

romántico romantic

romper v break

la ropa clothing; ~ **interior** underwear

rosa pink

roto broken

el rugby rugby

la rueda tire [tyre BE]; ~ **pinchada** flat tire [tyre BE]

las ruinas ruins

la ruta route; ~ **de senderismo** walking route

S

la sábana sheet

el sacacorchos corkscrew

el saco de dormir sleeping bag

la sala room; ~ **de conciertos** concert hall; ~ **de espera** waiting room; ~ **de reuniones** meeting room

la salida check-out (hotel)

la salida n exit; ~ **de urgencia** emergency exit

las salidas departures (airport)

salir v exit, leave

el salón room; ~ **de congresos** convention hall; ~ **de juegos recreativos** arcade; ~ **de manicura** nail salon

¡Salud! Cheers!

la salud health

las sandalias sandals

sangrar v bleed

la sangre blood

el santuario shrine

la sartén frying pan

la sauna sauna

el secador de pelo hair dryer

la secreción discharge (bodily fluid)

la seda silk

sediento thirsty

la seguridad security

el seguro insurance

seguro safe (protected)

el sello n stamp (postage)

el semáforo traffic light

la semana week

semanal weekly

el seminario seminar

el sendero trail; ~ **para bicicletas** bike route

el seno breast

sentarse v sit

separado separated (marriage)

ser v be

serio serious

el servicio restroom [toilet BE]; ~ service (in a restaurant); ~ **completo** full-service; ~ **de habitaciones** room service; ~ **inalámbrico a internet** wireless internet service; ~ **de internet** internet service; ~ **de lavandería** laundry service; ~ **de limpieza de habitaciones** housekeeping service

la servilleta napkin

sí yes

el sida AIDS

la silla chair; ~ **para niños** child seat; ~ **de ruedas** wheelchair

el símbolo symbol (keyboard)

sin without; ~ **alcohol** non-alcoholic; ~ **grasa** fat free; ~ **receta** over the counter (medication)

la sinagoga synagogue

el sitio de interés attraction (place)

el sobre envelope

el socorrista lifeguard

el sol sun

solamente only

soleado sunny

solo alone

soltero single (marriage)

el sombrero hat

la somnolencia drowsiness

sordo deaf

soso bland

el suavizante conditioner

el subtítulo subtitle

sucio dirty

la sudadera sweatshirt

el suelo floor

el sujetador bra

súper super (fuel)

superior upper

el supermercado grocery store, supermarket

la supervisión supervision

el sur south

el surfista windsurfer

T

la tabla board; **~ de snowboard** snowboard; **~ de surf** surfboard

la talla size; **~ grande** plus size; **~ pequeña** petite size

el taller garage (repair)

el talón de equipaje luggage [baggage BE] ticket

el tampón tampon

la taquilla locker; **~** reservation desk

tarde late (time)

la tarde afternoon

la tarjeta card; **~ de cajero automático** ATM card; **~ de crédito** credit card; **~ de débito** debit card; **~ de embarque** boarding pass; **~ internacional de estudiante** international student card; **~ de memoria** memory card; **~ de negocios** business card; **~ postal** postcard; **~ de seguro** insurance card; **~ de socio** membership card; **~ telefónica** phone card

la tasa fee

el taxi taxi

la taza cup; **~ medidora** measuring cup

el teatro theater; **~ de la ópera** opera house

la tela impermeable groundcloth [groundsheet BE]

el teleférico cable car

el teléfono telephone; **~ móvil** cell [mobile BE] phone; **~ público** pay phone

la telesilla chair lift

el telesquí ski/drag lift

la televisión TV

el templo temple (religious)

temprano early

el tenedor fork

tener v have; **~ dolor** v hurt (have pain); **~ náuseas** v be nauseous

el tenis tennis

la tensión arterial blood pressure

la terminal terminal (airport)

terminar v end

la terracotta terracotta

terrible terrible

el texto n text (message)

el tiempo time; **~** weather

la tienda store; **~ de alimentos naturales** health food store; **~ de antigüedades** antique store; **~ de bebidas alcohólicas** liquor store [off-licence BE]; **~ de campaña** tent; **~ de deportes** sporting goods store; **~ de fotografía** camera store; **~ de juguetes** toy store; **~ de música** music store; **~ de recuerdos** souvenir store; **~ de regalos** gift shop; **~ de ropa** clothing store

las tijeras scissors

la tintorería dry cleaner

el tipo de cambio exchange rate

tirar v pull (door sign)

la tirita bandage

la toalla towel

la toallita baby wipe

el tobillo ankle

el torneo de golf golf tournament

la torre tower

la tos n cough

toser v cough

el total total (amount)

trabajar v work

tradicional traditional

traducir v translate

traer v bring

tragar v swallow

el traje suit

tranquilo quiet

el tren train; **~ rápido** express train

triste sad

la trona highchair

el trozo piece

la tumbona deck chair

el turista tourist

U

último last

la universidad university

uno one

la uña nail; **~ del dedo** fingernail; **~ del pie** toenail

urgente urgent

usar v use

V

las vacaciones vacation [holiday BE]

vaciar v empty

la vacuna vaccination

la vagina vagina

la validez valid

valioso valuable

el valle valley

el valor value

el vaquero denim

los vaqueros jeans

el vaso glass (drinking)

el váter químico chemical toilet

vegetariano vegetarian

la vejiga bladder

vender v sell

el veneno poison

venir *v* come
la ventana window
el ventilador fan (appliance)
ver *v* see
verde green
el vestido dress (piece of clothing)
el viaje trip
el vidrio glass (material)

viejo old
la viña vineyard
la violación *n* rape
violar *v* rape
el visado visa (passport document)
visitar *v* visit
la vitamina vitamin
la vitrina display case
viudo widowed
vivir *v* live

vomitar *v* vomit
el vuelo flight; ~ **internacional** international flight; ~ **nacional** domestic flight

Z

la zapatería shoe store
las zapatillas slippers; ~ **de deporte** sneaker
los zapatos shoes
la zona area; ~ **de compras** shopping area; ~ **de fumadores** smoking area; ~ **para picnic** picnic area
el zoológico zoo
zurcir *v* mend

INDEX

pocket guide

MENORCA

Fifth Edition 2018

Editor: Helen Fanthorpe
Authors: Pam Barrett and Maciej Zglinicki
Head of Production: Rebeka Davies
Picture Editor: Tom Smyth
Cartography Update: Carte
Update Production: Apa Digital
Photography Credits: Alamy 7L, 13, 43, 89;
Bigstock 28, 99; Fotolia 7R, 11, 36; Getty
Images 4MC, 4TL, 5M, 6R, 64; iStock 26, 52,
65, 77, 92, 93, 96; Menorca Tourist Board
5TC, 16, 38, 41, 48, 54, 66, 68, 72, 76, 79,
80, 82, 84, 87, 88, 91, 94, 100, 102; Michael
Zegers/imageBROKER/REX/Shutterstock
19; Shutterstock 5T, 5MC, 5MC, 6L, 15, 20,
30, 31, 32, 44, 46, 57, 59, 62, 75; SuperStock
1, 4TC, 4ML, 5M, 24, 35, 50, 61, 70, 105;
TopFoto 23
Cover Picture: iStock

Distribution
UK, Ireland and Europe: Apa Publications
(UK) Ltd; sales@insightguides.com
United States and Canada: Ingram
Publisher Services; ips@ingramcontent.com
Australia and New Zealand: Woodslane;
info@woodslane.com.au
Southeast Asia: Apa Publications (SN) Pte;
singaporeoffice@insightguides.com
Worldwide: Apa Publications (UK) Ltd;
sales@insightguides.com

**Special Sales, Content Licensing
and CoPublishing**
Insight Guides can be purchased in bulk
quantities at discounted prices. We can
create special editions, personalised jackets
and corporate imprints tailored to your
needs. sales@insightguides.com;
www.insightguides.biz

Contact us
Every effort has been made to provide
accurate information in this publication,
but changes are inevitable. The publisher
cannot be responsible for any resulting loss,
inconvenience or injury. We would appreciate
it if readers would call our attention to any
errors or outdated information. We also
welcome your suggestions; please contact
us at: berlitz@apaguide.co.uk
www.insightguides.com/berlitz

Berlitz®

speaking your language

phrase book & dictionary
phrase book & CD

Available in: Arabic, Brazilian Portuguese*, Burmese*, Cantonese Chinese, Croatian, Czech*, Danish*, Dutch, English, Filipino, Finnish*, French, German, Greek, Hebrew*, Hindi*, Hungarian*, Indonesian, Italian, Japanese, Korean, Latin American Spanish, Malay, Mandarin Chinese, Mexican Spanish, Norwegian, Polish, Portuguese, Romanian*, Russian, Spanish, Swedish, Thai, Turkish, Vietnamese
*Book only